Praise for and Quotes by Paul Frey

"Paul's story is one that is worth telling because it never could have been predicted."

—DANIEL LICHTI
Bass Baritone and Professor of Voice

"There was no sweeter sound than four-part harmony coming from a Mennonite congregation."

—PAUL FREY

"I decided that I wanted to pursue opera full-time. I didn't know how I was going to go about it, and I wasn't sure how this was going to work out with my truck company. But I knew that it was something I absolutely had to do."

—PAUL FREY
1973

"He was virtually a music illiterate when I met him . . . So he learned by rote. And this made him insecure far longer than he should have been."

—HOWARD DYCK
Former Conductor of the
Kitchener-Waterloo Philharmonic Orchestra

"My major memories of Paul were his immense insecurities about his musical abilities. He'd have difficulties finding the notes and he took longer than most to master them. But every so often, this beautiful, wonderful sound would show itself and you could see what he was capable of."

—RAFFI ARMENIAN
Former Conductor of the
Kitchener-Waterloo Symphony Orchestra

"Well into my first year, I still couldn't read music; I couldn't count three beats to the bar and I couldn't read or understand French. So the 'dumb tenor label' stuck. And it wasn't pleasant."

—PAUL FREY
1977

"I didn't think then, nor do I think now, that the [University of Toronto Opera] School encouraged me or did much for me. I fell by their wayside."

—PAUL FREY

"I knew right away that this was the right guy for my *Lohengrin*. I thought to myself: 'there's something solid about this man. He's a thoroughly no-nonsense guy. I can get along fine with this guy. He's no *prima donna*.'"

—WERNER HERZOG
Film and Opera Director

"No, no. We want you!"

—WOLFGANG WAGNER
Director of the Bayreuth Wagnerian Festival
to Paul Frey on hearing him sing *Lohengrin* in Mannheim, Germany

"Paul Frey's Mannheim performance has instantly placed him among the world's great Wagnerians."

—KRISTIN MARIE GUIGUET
Music Magazine

"Suddenly every crowned head of European opera was buying a ticket for this performance, especially to hear Paul Frey sing."

—KRISTIN MARIE GUIGUET
Music Magazine

"It was just go-go-go during these years. I had come to opera late and it had come with a lot of struggle. So I'd need to make the very most of the time. There was no wasting time, as an opera singer's career is a long one."

—PAUL FREY
1987

"Paul Frey's performance [in Bayreuth] was everything that should be expected from the most important tenor to emerge since Vickers."

—KRISTIN MARIE GUIGUET
Music Magazine

"[Recalling his first performance at the Metropolitan Opera:] My heart was pounding so much, I thought it would come through my chest. I was having a panic attack."

—PAUL FREY
1987

"Paul Frey is an astonishing yet hidden asset for Canada! His incredible tenor voice, commanding stage presence, and mastery of Wagner's *Lohengrin* repertoire deserve to be rediscovered. A hidden treasure in Canadian musical history!"

—ADRIENNE CLARKSON
Former Governor General of Canada;
author of *Room for All of Us*

Paul Frey:
A Story Never Predicted

Paul Frey:
A Story Never Predicted

From Trucking to the World Opera Stage

Nancy Silcox

Foreword by Werner Herzog

WIPF & STOCK · Eugene, Oregon

PAUL FREY: A STORY NEVER PREDICTED
From Trucking to the World Opera Stage

Copyright © 2020 Nancy Silcox. All rights reserved. Except for brief quotations in critical publications or reviews, no part of this book may be reproduced in any manner without prior written permission from the publisher. Write: Permissions, Wipf and Stock Publishers, 199 W. 8th Ave., Suite 3, Eugene, OR 97401.

Wipf & Stock
An Imprint of Wipf and Stock Publishers
199 W. 8th Ave., Suite 3
Eugene, OR 97401

www.wipfandstock.com

PAPERBACK ISBN: 978-1-7252-6165-5
HARDCOVER ISBN: 978-1-7252-6164-8
EBOOK ISBN: 978-1-7252-6166-2

Manufactured in the U.S.A. 06/17/20

*This book is dedicated to my husband,
Louis Silcox, who keeps house and home together
while I tell stories that need to be told.*

You are born an artist or you are not. And you stay an artist, dear, even if your voice is less of a fireworks. The artist is always there.
—MARIA CALLAS, OPERA SOPRANO

If one has not heard Wagner at Bayreuth, *one has heard nothing!* Take lots of handkerchiefs because you will cry a great deal! Also take a sedative because you will be exalted to the point of delirium!
—GABRIEL FAURÉ (1845-1924), FRENCH COMPOSER, LETTER, 1884

Contents

Foreword by Werner Herzog	xi
Preface	xv

Part 1: Swiss-Mennonite Roots: Coming to Religious Freedom   1

    1. Frey and Luther   3
    2. Mennonites to Ontario   6
    3. John and Lucinda Frey   8

Part 2: Church, Work, and Music: In That Order   11

    4. An Unremarkable Childhood   13
    5. Upward and Onward   16
    6. Just the Way It Is   18
    7. Rethinking His Priorities   20
    8. To Baptize or Not to Baptize   22
    9. The Arrangement   24

Part 3: Making Room for Music   27

    10. The Glad Tidings Quartet   29
    11. The Schneider Male Chorus   32
    12. Coming of Age   35
    13. At a Musical Crossroads   38

Part 4: Music, Then Everything Else   41

    14. A Musical Star Comes to Town   43
    15. The Summer Music Workshop   45
    16. Putting the Puzzle Together   50
    17. A Cautionary Word from a Star   53

Part 5: Opera School: Odd Man Out — 57

    18. Picking Up the Pieces — 59
    19. Back to School — 62
    20. More Moonlighting — 66
    21. Opera School Encore — 70
    22. A Turning Point — 73
    23. An American Road Trip — 77
    24. Back to the Status Quo — 79

Part 6: European Adventure: Steeling Himself to Fail — 81

    25. The Canada Council Offers a Chance — 83
    26. One of Five — 86
    27. Finishing What He Had Started — 89
    28. Sorting It Out — 92
    29. Ten-Month Home Interlude — 96

Part 7: A New Life in Basel — 99

    30. On Their Way — 101
    31. Getting Settled and Learning the Ropes — 103
    32. Bargaining with the Boss — 106
    33. Settling In for the Long Run — 108
    34. Some Constructive Criticism — 111
    35. Time Zone Mayhem — 113
    36. Three of Three — 116

Part 8: Branching Out — 125

    37. Radio Gigs — 127
    38. Into Germany — 129
    39. Italian Adventure — 132

Part 9: Next Five Years—Basel? Or Elsewhere? — 135

    40. Tenure for Life? — 137
    41. A Shock Becomes a Blessing — 141
    42. A Perfect Match — 144

Part 10: Richard Wagner and Beyond — 147

    43. A Condensed Wagner Primer — 149
    44. Lohengrin, Karlsruhe — 155

45. Somebody Important in the Audience	157
46. Mannheim	160
47. Bigger and Bigger	165
48. Traveling, Traveling Everywhere	168

Part 11: Lohengrin in Bayreuth — **171**

49. Being Lohengrin	173
50. Working, Working . . .	176
51. Dealing with Fame	180

Part 12: After Lohengrin: On Top of the Opera World — **183**

52. No Rest for This Tenor	185
53. To the Top: The Met	187
54. It Has to Be 150 Percent	190
55. An Invitation with a Difference	193

Part 13: A Career Disappointment and a Well-Deserved Honor — **197**

56. Strike Out for Canada	199
57. A Dark Cloud over the Met	202
58. Before I Get Too Old	205
59. An Honor Bestowed	208
Epilogue: Back Where He Started	210
Endnotes	*213*
Bibliography	*217*

Foreword

FALL 1986 SAW ME on a fact-finding mission. I'd been sent to the *Badisches Staatstheater* (opera house) in Karlsruhe, Germany to listen to a Canadian singing the lead role in Richard Wagner's opera *Lohengrin*.

The story why is worth retelling. Wolfgang Wagner, who was, at the time, director of the Bayreuth, Germany *Festspielehaus*, had been searching for a new tenor to sing *Lohengrin* for his Bayreuth's summer *Festspiele*. He'd heard that there was a Canadian, a man named Paul Frey, who was good—very good—and he was performing in the same role at Karlsruhe.

And, as I was to be the director of *Lohengrin* the following summer at Bayreuth, Wagner wanted my opinion whether this Frey fellow had the right stuff.

That I, a feature film maker, would be able to judge the suitability of an opera singer was not entirely right, and not entirely wrong. I had just finished a film in the jungles of Amazonia, where I had moved a big steamboat over a mountain with the help of over a thousand tribal extras. I'd also worked with a nightmare of a leading actor who was borderline insane. This assignment paled to that.

In between film projects, I had also been literally dragged into directing an opera, Busoni's *Doktor Faust*, at the *Teatro Comunale* in Bologna, Italy. It was on the strength of that production, my first ever opera, that Wagner did his best to convince me to dip my toes into the deep waters of Richard Wagner at Bayreuth.

I had flatly refused in the beginning, but once I listened to the *Vorspiel*, the overture of *Lohengrin*, the opera Wagner planned for the summer season of 1987, I immediately knew this was big. So big that I had no choice. I accepted the assignment.

Now Bayreuth was looking for a new face to fill the role of a mystic who arrives in a troubled land to save a princess in distress. That the savior arrives for his mission in a boat pulled by a swan, and can only accomplish his task if he remains nameless, adds mystery to the tale.

Wagner had been hearing positive things about a Canadian tenor named Paul Frey, who'd been, for some time, a contract singer at the *Stadttheatre Basel*. But now Frey was breaking through to the top-flight opera houses. His recent fill-in role for Peter Hofmann's *Lohengrin* in Mannheim had the opera world suddenly looking his way.

Mr. Frey would be reprising the role in Karlsruhe. And so, Wolfgang Wagner wanted me to see if this Canadian was up to par for Bayreuth, an opera house his grandfather Richard Wagner had designed for bold innovative stagings.

Of Paul Frey I knew little: a Canadian; his unusual background as an agricultural truck driver who could not read musical scores; his voice: a resonant, powerful tenor.

Thirty-five years after the performance, I vividly remember the moment I first set eyes on him in Karlsruhe.

Elevated above the stage, Lohengrin steps out of his swan boat and makes his way towards the front. After a few steps, the entire fifteen-foot-high background of wooden scenery collapsed, crashing down behind the arriving Swan Prince.

The audience gasped. Paul Frey, unfazed, didn't miss a note. The magic coming from this singular Lohengrin's throat remained clear, strong, and true, despite the mayhem.

It was in this moment that I knew I had my man.

My feelings were only strengthened as Paul and I spoke after the conclusion of the opera. As I had grown up in a remote mountain valley in Bavaria, I was curious about his childhood on a farm in Canada. He spoke to me about his job driving farm animals to market—and singing along to Elvis on the radio!

Anybody who can milk a cow and load pigs to go to market, I thought, is a solid human being with a different, rich inner landscape.

I also got the feeling that this opera singer, like me, understanding the greatness of Wagner's music, was not one of the quasi-religious fanatics about the composer himself. He didn't ascribe to Bayreuth as the Holy Grail of opera. This was a no-nonsense kind of guy. I knew that he and I would work very well together.

Foreword

When he shared with me that he had struggled learning to read music, my feeling that he was a kindred spirit only deepened. I confided that I couldn't read music either! I returned to Bayreuth and informed Wolfgang Wagner of my feelings.

Later, when I was informed that indeed Paul Frey would be our star Lohengrin, I was delighted.

Rehearsals for *Lohengrin* began around six weeks before we opened. And I have only fond memories of this time. Some amusing memories too—one involving Peter Schneider, Bayreuth's esteemed musical conductor.

At Bayreuth, the orchestra pit, where the orchestra and conductor are positioned, is covered. The audience cannot see the orchestra at all, although from the stage they are visible.

During one rehearsal, I wanted to make an ironic point about the "sanctity" of this opera house, a feeling that had worn on the nerves of everyone working hard there. And so, I called out: "Herr Schneider, this is a moment when we should change the light. Could you stop the band!" THE BAND!

All I could hear from the pit were shouts of delight, laughter, and slapping of thighs. From this moment on, the orchestra loved me.

As I hoped it would be, the 1986 production of *Lohengrin* at the Bayreuth Summer Wagnerian Festival was a tremendous success. It made Paul Frey a world star. And a star he surely was. Still, under the role of pure fantasy was a solid, real man.

I have only fond memories of that wonderful summer we shared so many years ago.

Werner Herzog
Los Angeles

Preface

IN 2016, I'D BEEN requested by a small high school in the town of Elmira, just north of Waterloo, Ontario, Canada, to write an anthology of the abundance of successful alumni who had attended the school over the years. Given Elmira District Secondary School's reputation as a producer of academic, literary, athletic, and entertainment stars, I jumped at the chance.

Among the list of subjects that the school had provided me for possible inclusion in the book were a number of national and international celebrities. They included best-selling authors Malcolm Gladwell and Roger Martin, NHL players Rod Seiling and the late Dan Snyder, NHL referee Garrett Rank, *Murdoch Mysteries* actor Kate Greenhouse, *Homeless Jesus* sculptor Tim Schmalz, and Canadian Screen Awards animator Sarah Mercey.

And Paul Frey . . . "music," the notation said.

"Paul Frey," I pondered. "I know that name. A classical singer, I think. Maybe opera?"

As I whittled down the list and approached a Frey interview, I began to do my homework. Surprisingly, the internet provided a number of references:

> *Born and raised in a conservative order Mennonite farm family, a high school drop-out, worked in his family trucking company driving hogs and cows to market. Started singing with a faith-based quartet in the Waterloo area then moved on to sing with a community men's choir.*

"Unique background for an opera singer, I wagered . . ."

> *Turned towards opera and was admitted to the University of Toronto Opera School.*

"With a Grade 9 education? There's a story here."

Preface

Sang with famed contralto Maureen Forrester while at U. of T. but left Opera School never having sung a lead part in a 3-act opera.

"Whoa! What happened here?"

Won a spot in a Canada Council audition tour of European opera houses and was hired by the Basel Opera House as a house tenor.

"Basel certainly saw something Canada hadn't..."

Filled in for the ailing star Peter Hofmann in Munich and from that appearance won the lead in the opera Lohengrin at the 1987 Bayreuth Festival.

"Now this is getting exciting..."

Became a world star, singing at the Metropolitan Opera House, Covent Garden in London, England, La Scala in Milan and the Vienna State Opera House. Considered by many opera experts to be among the finest tenors in the world.

Retired to rural Waterloo in 2005.

"After jet-setting the world? I bet that wasn't easy."

The research had left me astounded, prompting me to wonder, "why has no one written this fascinating man's biography before?"

It was in this frame of mind that I arrived in 2017 at the Frey home in St. Clements, north of Waterloo, to interview Paul Frey for the school anthology.

"Why has no one written my biography?" chuckled the soft-spoken and youthful Frey, now in his late seventies. "Well, I haven't seen much interest in opera around the St. Clements post office or the general store!" he joked.

The next couple of hours, as I filled in bits and pieces of what surely had been a remarkable life, only convinced me of the need to correct a monumental oversight. Paul Frey's was a story like no other—a testament to talent and perseverance, disappointment and good fortune, with a hearty helping of hard, hard, hard work.

A telephone call to Daniel Lichti, Professor of Voice at Wilfrid Laurier University and Paul's colleague at Opera School, only added to my desire to fully tell the Frey story. "Paul's has been a remarkable life," stated Lichti, "because it could never have been predicted."

And so, one year later, biographer and opera star embarked on a life story, one that had begun portentously in 1548 with one Johannes Frey,

Preface

traveling from Basel, Switzerland to Germany to meet Martin Luther! It then crossed an ocean more than three centuries later as a number of Freys joined other disaffected Swiss Mennonites seeking freedom to worship and land to farm in a pioneer Waterloo County.

Over the ensuing sixteen months of interviews for the book, and untold hours of writing the Frey story, never did I fail to give thanks that this remarkable story was mine to share.

———

As opera star Paul Frey enters his ninth decade in 2021, he remains largely a product of his lineage: understated and modest, proud yet humble, supremely talented and sincere—a private man who led a very public life.

Stories of life behind the stage curtain abound in *Paul Frey: A Story Never Predicted. From Trucking to the World Opera Stage.* Canadian opera stars Maureen Forrester, Louis Quilico, Jon Vickers, and Ben Heppner take their place alongside world stars Placido Domingo and Peter Hofmann. Legendary composers Richard Wagner, Richard Strauss, and Franz Liszt also play their appointed roles. And outside the operatic world, notables German Chancellor Helmut Kohl, former Canadian Governor-General Adrienne Clarkson, and revered film director Werner Herzog drop by too. A fine tale for sure!

Nancy Silcox
New Hamburg, Ontario

Part 1

Swiss-Mennonite Roots:
Coming to Religious Freedom

(1772–1941)

1

Frey and Luther

LIVING IN BASEL, SWITZERLAND between 1978 and 2005, Canadian Paul Frey decided to do some genealogical digging. He was aware that his Swiss-Mennonite forbearers had come to southwestern Ontario, Canada around 1850. Beyond that, he knew little else. Taking advantage of the serendipity of his present Swiss residence, Paul made plans to visit a distant relative, one Johannes Frey, living in Germany. Through previous correspondence, Paul was aware that Johannes knew a fair amount about the Frey family history. And he might open that door to the past.

"Johannes took me to the original Frey farm near Sinsheim, in the southwest area of Germany," Paul recalled. "It was from here that, supposedly, my ancestors had set out for Ontario so many generations before."

Returning home to Basel more interested in his heritage than when he had left, Paul was now inspired to dig deeper. He'd had in his possession the hitherto unopened *Genealogy of the Frey Family from 1772 to 1965*. Written in 1934 by Levi B. Frey, and continued after his death in 1956 by his niece Elizabeth Wideman, the book answered more of Paul's questions. It revealed some surprises and an astounding historical meeting.

The preface began:

> In 1529 from the 1st to the 4th of October we find one Robert Frey (a lawyer from Basil[sic]) accompanied Ulrich Zwingli in Marburg with others to meet Martin Luther and his delegates to confer on matters of religion.[1]

Martin Luther! A compelling beginning to a family history indeed! These "matters of religion" were ones that would send Europe into ferment,

Part 1: Swiss-Mennonite Roots: Coming to Religious Freedom

influencing the lives of tens of thousands of Europeans living in Switzerland, Germany, Holland, England, and other nations during the tumultuous decades to come.

What role lawyer Robert Frey took in this auspicious meeting between Zwingli, a Swiss priest, and Luther is lost to history. Zwingli's actions after the journey are not. By 1520, he had initiated his own religious reforms in Switzerland and had gathered around him a number of followers, including one Conrad Grebel, the son of a wealthy Swiss merchant and an ordained minister.[2]

At the outset a fervent follower of Zwingli's reforming aims, by 1525 Grebel had broken away from his mentor. Among certain key areas of difference, Grebel passionately believed that baptism must only be undertaken by consenting adults, not children or infants. As such they were known as Anabaptists.

In the process of developing their religious philosophies, Grebel and his followers eventually came to see Luther and Zwingli as "halfway men," prone to compromise. Grebel's Anabaptists sought not to *reform* religion but to restore the religious ideal. That was Christianity as set out in the New Testament.

Zwingli and the Zurich city council reacted swiftly against Grebel and his Anabaptists. Many of them fled—some to the Alsace Region, others to the Palatinate, in southwest Germany. A group led by Jacob Hutter sought refuge in Moravia (Czechoslovakia).[3] They would come to be known as Hutterites. Still others, led by former Roman Catholic priest Menno Simons, escaped further north to the Netherlands. These Menists became the Mennonites.[4]

Religious persecution of the Mennonites and Hutterites flared again during The Thirty Years' War, a brutal conflict that razed the German landscape between the years 1618 and 1648. Hostilities had originally erupted when Ferdinand II, king of Bohemia, had initiated measures to wipe out Protestantism in his kingdom. Protestants reacted violently and widespread sectarian violence ensued. Philosophically, as pacifists, the Anabaptists took no part in these religious wars. However, as visible minorities, they were again the target of persecution.

Followers of Hutter, who had been granted religious freedom in Moravia a century before, witnessed this clemency rescinded. Thousands of Hutterites fled to Transylvania and Hungary. Further to the north, Menno

Simons and his Mennonite followers fared only slightly better. Still, a number of their settlements were razed to the ground.[5]

The end of the Thirty Years' War in 1648 saw Protestants and Roman Catholics given their freedom to worship in the faith of their choice. Fortune smiled briefly for the Anabaptists too when King Ludwig of Germany granted them refugee status in return for rebuilding the devastated countryside and economy.

This good fortune was short-lived. With Ludwig's death, the amnesty ended and religious persecutions commenced again. With Europe a battleground, Swiss, German, and Dutch Mennonites and Hutterites packed up their lives to begin again in America. The first settlement of Swiss Mennonites to eastern Pennsylvania began in 1707, continuing into the 1750s.

2

Mennonites to Ontario

AFTER THE DISRUPTION OF the American Civil War, a number of Mennonites left settlements in Pennsylvania, heading north to British North America. In 1786, the first migrants settled in the Niagara Peninsula at Twenty Mile Creek, familiarly called "The Twenty."[6]

Over 1799–1800, a larger migration of Pennsylvania Mennonites, led by Joseph Schoerg and Samuel Betzner, carried on past "The Twenty" to the Indian-settled lands of Waterloo County, west of Lake Ontario. Judging the soil fertile (presently under thousands of acres of virgin forest), with the slow-flowing Grand River a source of fresh water, they set up camp. The settlement was first called Sandhills for the sand dunes in the area.[7] In 1807, Sandhills was renamed Eby's Town (Ebytown) to honor its first Mennonite bishop, Benjamin Eby.[8]

To the northwest of Ebytown lay the fledgling townships of Woolwich, Wellesley, and Wilmot.[9] Largely unsettled by Europeans three decades after Schoerg and Betzner founded Ebytown, they were sparsely occupied by indigenous people.

An adventure-seeking English Loyalist from Vermont, Captain Thomas Smith is recorded as the first identified immigrant to have settled in these areas.[10] Smith may have arrived as early as 1807, setting up shelter near what is now Winterbourne in Woolwich Township. He is credited with establishing a stage service that ran to Berlin and Preston between 1830 and 1850.[11]

By 1837, American Mennonites and Amish as well as Germans, Dutch, French, and British were moving into these uncharted lands. By 1860, in Woolwich, the earliest tract settled, a number of well-established communities had developed. They included Elmira, Winterbourne, Conestogo, and St. Jacobs.

It is into this fledgling rural community at this time in history that Paul Frey's great-great-grandfather Johannes Frey arrived from Germany. Like his Mennonite and Amish brothers, Johannes was bound and determined to forge a better life for himself and his family.

Paul's Frey pilgrimage to his ancestor's hometown in Sinsheim in the late twentieth century paid tribute to the pioneer spirit of Johannes Frey and those who came after. Genealogical research places Paul as the seventh generation of the Frey family and the third generation to be born in Waterloo County.[12]

3

John and Lucinda Frey

BORN INTO OLD ORDER Mennonite families, John Hoffman Frey (April 6, 1906) and Lucinda Bauman Brubacher (March 1, 1908) had followed the conservative traditions of their faith throughout their youth and young adulthood. As was the tradition, both had left school after eighth grade. John, born to a family of twelve children, would assist his father on the farm. Lucinda, one of only three children, worked in the family home. And, if time allowed, she'd "work out" in neighbors' homes, providing childcare and engaged in house and kitchen work.

Church fellowship joined family life as the primary focus of a young Mennonite's life. Paul describes what would have been a typical Sunday at an Old Order Mennonite home. "My parents, like most Mennonites, didn't go to the same meeting house [church] for each Sunday service. There were a number of these houses of worship around the area and people might go to this one one week, then that one another. Depending on the meeting house, people could attend morning, afternoon, or evening services."

"But one tradition was a constant," says Paul. "After any one of the services, people would drop in on their friends and neighbors to have a meal. No invitation needed. So, of course, people had to be prepared to feed their guests."

As was the case with most of their peers, John Frey and Lucinda Brubacher likely met in the church community. They surely courted at the Sunday evening "Times" get-togethers. These social events allowed young people to meet and, in many cases, choose a mate. John was twenty-three and Lucinda twenty-one when they married (November 14, 1929). The

John and Lucinda Frey

couple welcomed their first child, Edna, on September 5, 1930. Amsey, their first son, followed on June 16, 1932.

Within a short time, the Freys purchased a 100-acre farm southwest of St. Jacobs. The price was $8,000. Given the times and the growing economic Depression, such a major purchase was significant and speaks to the thrift of the Old Order Mennonites. Still, moving through the early 1930s, even thrift couldn't outweigh the far-reaching effects of the economic downturn.

With the cost of feed for cattle high, and the price paid for grain, corn, and other agricultural crops low, John realized he wasn't going to support a wife and two children with the present situation. The Frey farm went up for sale and the family relocated to a smaller and less-expensive operation outside the village of Heidelberg. "Dad felt a $5,000 operation was more within their means," says Paul.

And how do horse-and-buggy Mennonites move households in the dead of winter? "By horse-drawn sleigh," Paul offers. "And my mother was pregnant at the same time!" The Frey family welcomed their third child, Lena, in February 5, 1934. Alice followed on April 20, 1938.

Sometime between 1934 and 1938, a significant philosophical shift occurred in the Frey family, one which would ultimately change the course of Paul Frey's life. One raw and blustery Ontario winter Sunday, John had hitched up the family horse, attached it to the buggy, and prepared to drive to the Sunday meeting house service. He was in a foul mood.

What Lucinda was not privy to that fateful morning was that her husband had become increasingly unhappy with the Sunday ritual. Church wasn't the problem; the horse was. "My father wanted to drive a car, not a horse," offers Paul. He relates the family lore, told by his older sister Edna, which contributed to John Frey getting his life-altering wish.

"They were late and the weather was getting worse. Apparently, part-way there, Dad abruptly stopped the horse, turned the buggy around, and headed back home. My mother was startled and asked Dad what was going on. 'We wouldn't have been late if we were driving a car instead of a horse,' Dad barked."

Sometime after the trauma, John Frey bought his car. He retired his horses and the Frey family made plans to leave the Old Order. As monumental a shift as this was, it was not unheard of in the community—especially given the times. Other fundamentalists had chosen to realign their faith to join the Markham Mennonites. Less severe in their lifestyle than the Old Orders, the Markhams were allowed to own and drive a car—albeit

Part 1: Swiss-Mennonite Roots: Coming to Religious Freedom

black, with no chrome embellishment. Other Old Order practices, including abjuring hydro and modern conveniences, remained.

But now that change was in the air, Lucinda made known her own wishes. "Mother wanted her children to be able to go to Sunday school," explains Paul, "but the Markhams didn't allow this." And so John and Lucinda Frey joined the moderate St. Jacobs Mennonite Church. John had his beloved car, the Frey children were able to attend Sundays, and everyone was satisfied.

Despite the conversion, Lucinda Frey didn't alter her style of dress. She continued to wear the cape dress (a modest bosom-covering style) and the white muslin head covering. John modified his style of dress only slightly, wearing a navy blue suit for church and special events, instead of the requisite black.

And the basic tenets of the Mennonite faith remained as they had been over generations of the Frey family. Living *in* the world, not *of* the world, was paramount in these ideological beliefs. As such, Mennonites would abide by the laws, customs, ways, and means of the majority; however, they would not philosophically nor practically follow suit. Pacifism, non-violence, and non-participation in armed conflict would guide the Mennonites through the hurly-burly of the world outside their doors. "Service to others" would guide their social compass.

Part 2

Church, Work, and Music: In That Order

(1941–1961)

4

An Unremarkable Childhood

A CURLY-HAIRED REDHEAD, WITH freckles and packing a bundle of energy, Paul Frey recalls his childhood as "unremarkable" and "happy." Born on April 20th, 1941, he'd remain the baby of the family until 1947, when Kenneth (Ken) was born. Harold, the Freys' last baby, born in 1949, died shortly after birth.

Paul's memories of growing up in a close-knit Mennonite farm family invariably involve outdoor adventure. One sees him, no more than three or four, at a barn-raising. With the assembled male volunteers taking a break for a hearty Mennonite lunch, and the women occupied with serving, an impish Paul took the occasion of climbing the ladder that reached up to the top of the barn rafters. "I doubt if I was scared; it was an adventure. But Dad was not pleased to have to bring me down," he chuckles. A sense of adventure would follow Paul throughout his life.

Another early memory finds Paul paddling in a creek that ran behind his house. He was tagging along with an older cousin. The lad possessed a talent that Paul greatly admired. "My cousin was a couple of years older than me and was an expert trapper. He'd set traps for muskrats along the creek and on that day was checking to see if he'd caught anything. I remember the excitement of coming across one trap and finding an animal in it." And while Paul doesn't remember the next step in the trapping process, he recalls proudly displaying a muskrat tail on the aerial of his bicycle.

Church played an integral part of young Paul's life. And while a young, spirited lad like himself might become drowsy during lengthy Sunday sermons, he wakened during an always-resounding hymn sing. "Women and girls were on one side of the church; men and boys were on the other. All hymns were *a capella*, in four-part harmony. There was no piano or organ accompaniment. Instead, a lead chorister got the congregation in tune using a pitch pipe."

Young Paul liked singing, if only for the reason that it broke up seemingly interminable sermons. Little could he have predicted, as a curly-mopped rascal, how much music would play a part in his life in the years to come.

In 1947, Paul began grade one at the two-room Heidelberg Public School. "Grades one to five in one room; the seniors from grade six to grade eight in the other," he recalls. Each day, accompanied by older sisters Lena, in grade seven, and Alice, in grade three, he'd head down the Freys' long driveway and walk the short trek along the highway to Heidelberg Public School. No yellow school busses in these days; no parent chauffeurs either.

Thanks to his older sisters, Paul hadn't begun his education at a disadvantage. "We only spoke Pennsylvania Dutch at home. But my older sisters made sure I knew some English." By this time, his older sister Edna, age sixteen, and his brother Amsey, age fourteen, had both left school. Conversion to the modern Mennonite faith hadn't (at that point) altered John and Lucinda Frey's belief that children should leave school after grade eight or at age fourteen.[13]

And while Paul's memories of those early days are few, he does recall, with horror, what his mother had chosen for his first day of school. "They were three-quarter-length pants—not shorts, not full length. They cut off at my knees and I hated them!" His usual garb was what he calls "chesterfield overalls." "My mom used the fabric from an old couch—a chesterfield to make us our school pants," he says, with a laugh.

The students who made up Heidelberg Public School came from a mixture of faiths—Mennonite, Lutheran, and Baptist. They were of varied economic backgrounds too—some "village kids," with parents who worked in stores or factories, but most of them from farm backgrounds.

The school was heated by a coal-burning furnace and it wasn't unusual during the cold winter months for an enterprising youngster to bring a roasting potato from home. Sometime before lunch Paul might make an excuse to head to the basement of the school. There he'd open the door of the furnace and place a baking potato strategically inside. By lunch time: "Yum. With butter. Terrific!" he reminisces.

Every so often, the custodian would clean out the coal eater and pile the cinders behind the school. It was another fine opportunity for the

Heidelberg young bucks. "The pile was so high you could get your bike going as fast as you could pedal it, head up the hill of cinders, and fly off the top." Paul shakes his head and grins at the memory.

With a sense of fun and of an outgoing nature, Paul had no problems finding his peer group. He'd palled up with Roy Hoffman and Robert Schneider, both farm kids like himself. The trio would remain fast friends until they left elementary school. "We stuck together and nobody bullied us," recalls Paul.

Looking back at his performance during eight years of elementary school, Paul admits to a tendency of inattention of his teachers. "I loved to read as a kid, and always kept an open book in my desk. I'd slouch down, slide the book out, and read when I was supposed to be listening. I'm not sure how often I was caught, but I do remember my teacher grabbing me by my ear and twisting it when she caught me in the act."

Forty years later, during an interview for the CBC television program *Adrienne Clarkson Presents*, Paul is seen in conversation with one-time Heidelberg Public School Principal Don Poth. He admits to being strapped on at least two occasions. "My teacher strapped me above the wrist. It was against the rules, but in those days you didn't go home and complain about the teacher. You'd be just as likely to get another strapping from your parents for what you did."

5

Upward and Onward

A SIGNIFICANT CHANGE IN the Frey family's life occurred in 1949 when John bought a truck. His plan was to begin transporting livestock, driving his cattle and hogs to market instead of paying a company to do it. The purchase was a good investment too. Before long, neighbors hired him to ferry their own animals. John soon found out that he'd need a PCV license to legally be paid for this service and quickly took steps to conform to the technicality.

It should come as no surprise that a man who changed churches so he could drive a vehicle would love the feel of a truck under his control. And with "John H. Frey" painted on the side of his vehicle, John's satisfaction with the faith road he had taken was even greater.

There were more changes on the horizon too. In 1953, when Paul was twelve, a farmer with a large operation just north of St. Clements, a short distance from the Frey property in Heidelberg, was killed in a motor vehicle accident. The man's family now needed to sell his property. John Frey's brother Tillman bought it, with the plan that his oldest son, Paul's cousin Henry, eventually would run it. But the arrangement didn't work out and before long the two Frey brothers were involved in some real estate switching. Paul explains:

"It turns out the St. Clements farm was just too big for my cousin. They wondered if we could consider a trade. Dad would get the bigger property, and our farm in Heidelberg would go to them." John thought the trade was a good one but Lucinda was opposed. Property size had nothing to do with her protestations. At the time, St. Clements was primarily a Catholic village, with most of the residents attending the St. Clements

Catholic Church. These Catholics would be her children's playmates. No comforting thought for a conservative-order Mennonite mother!

More worrisome for Lucinda was that there was only one school in the village and that was St. Clements Separate School. "And there was no way my mother was going to let me and my younger brother Ken go to a Catholic School," explains Paul. The nearest elementary school would mean a lengthy bus ride from home. The conundrum was solved when the Frey boys were given permission to finish their school year at Heidelberg. Paul was in grade eight and was graduating from elementary school. Ken, in grade two, would need to change schools come September.

So everybody was happy in the upwardly mobile Frey family. The new farm was a step or two up from their present property. Paul recalls his amazement as a youth taking in the new "digs." "There was two of everything: two driveways; two gas pumps—one gas, one diesel; two silos. Inside the house there were two bathrooms. We even had a weigh scale for the trucks. Dad saw that for twenty-five cents neighbors could have the convenience of weighing their loads close to home."

Paul calls his father "ambitious." The "bigger is better" philosophy suited John Frey—and, for that matter, many Mennonite farmers. Religious conservatism could walk hand in hand with business success. "Men like my father were brought up thinking that success was measured in how much money you make, how big your farm was, how many vehicles you had. Families who didn't have these weren't considered successful." Even Old Orders who had eschewed modernity had their own way of touting success, advises Paul. "In the team of horses they drove—clean and brushed; in the size of the buggy they rode in; even in the way they tipped their hat."

In many ways, in years to come, Paul's philosophies of success would come to parallel his father's.

6

Just the Way It Is

John and Lucinda Frey may have left the severe ways of their ancestors behind as they embraced modern life of the mid-twentieth century, but philosophically one remnant of their Old Order heritage remained firm. Both boys and girls went to school until they turned fourteen or completed grade eight. Both Edna, born in 1930, and Amsey, born in 1932, had completed their schooling at the end of grade eight. Now Amsey assisted on the farm; Edna's role was house and garden work.

But by the time daughters Lena and Alice were born, John and Lucinda had moderated their ways towards education. Both girls were allowed to carry on into high school. But the boys, Paul and Ken, would toe the mark and end their schooling at fourteen. But far from leaving his sons adrift in the material world with scant education, John Frey had the futures of his three boys well thought out. Amsey would inherit the family farm. Paul would take over the transport trucking business. And Ken, the youngest, could have his choice: trucking or farming. John Frey would ensure that all his children were well provided for.[14]

Amsey had been agreeable to the plan, and by the time Paul reached his own fourteenth year, his older brother was well established, running one of the Frey's two farms. Dad's blueprint suited Paul as well. "I sure didn't see myself as a farmer, but a guy driving my own truck. That was just fine with me."

Graduating from grade eight in 1954, age thirteen years and two months, Paul needed to have attained his fourteenth birthday before he could legally put away the books. So it looked like he'd be going to high school—Elmira District Secondary School—come September. At least until he turned fourteen the next April.

So on the Tuesday following Labor Day of 1954, Paul Frey caught the high school bus. He calls that auspicious experience, and those days following it, "traumatizing." Much of the trauma, he admits had to do with the "relaxed" learning style he'd adopted throughout elementary school, and his academic unpreparedness for secondary learning. He's forthright about his significant academic failings. "I was not a good student. I'd never done homework throughout elementary school and hadn't really paid much attention to the teacher's lessons. I'd spent as much of my class time as I could reading the book I currently had hidden in my desk. So when I got to high school I really wasn't prepared at all."

On the other hand, he'd discovered school sports and thoroughly enjoyed this aspect of high school. "Basketball and track and field—pole vaulting especially." He'd loved to have joined a school team or two but that was out of the question. "I'd have had to miss the bus home because practices were after school. And nobody from home was going to drive in to pick me up after practice."

When exam time appeared on the horizon, young Paul found he was at a severe disadvantage. "I had no notes to study from. Who knew you were supposed to pay attention in class and take notes to help you study for exams!" So when exams were returned, Paul Frey was not among the brighter lights of the class. "In June, I was able to just barely scrape through in all my subjects except music. That I failed."

More than sixty years later, Paul Frey, world-class tenor, finds sweet irony in the situation.

7

Rethinking His Priorities

WORKING FOR HIS FATHER over that summer, Paul had occasion to reflect on the previous year's academic lessons. "I was a better student at the end of the year than I had been at the beginning. And I'd had lots of positive experiences. So I began to think that I'd like to go back and give grade ten a try." Admitting that the lure of school sports was more prominent than any wish to improve himself academically, he still surprised himself. "I sure wouldn't have predicted this in September."

But when he mentioned his thoughts to his parents, John Frey especially was adamant. "Dad felt I hadn't been serious enough in school to warrant going back. My failure in music was proof of that." No way would he have anything to do with his son continuing his education. Paul was needed on the delivery truck and that was that! John Frey stayed firm.

Paul felt determined enough about his wants and needs that he decided it was time to pull out the "heavy guns." "My mother knew how to manipulate my father, while all the time letting him think that he was making the big family decisions." So as the summer waned, and September approached, Lucinda Frey, as her son's champion, began to lobby her husband. Whether John Frey came to see his son's point of view or he'd simply grown weary of his wife's supplications will never be known. In any case, by the time trick-or-treaters were on the prowl, John had given in and offered his son the chance to return to school. Paul recalls his state of mind now that he'd finally achieved his goal.

"But by now, school had been in for two months. Given that I wasn't a great student to begin with, how could I catch up with my class half way

Rethinking His Priorities

through the first term? I knew I couldn't, and it would have turned out to be a bad experience. So I declined. I was out of school for good."

Paul Frey, age fourteen, was an official school dropout. "It didn't upset me that much. I knew that what was ahead of me would be fine." "Fine" meant that after a period of time working alongside his father and learning the fine points of running John H. Frey Trucking, Paul would inherit the business.

For the present, he'd ride along as a helper on one of the three trucks when John or his drivers did livestock pickups and deliveries. He'd get a chance to do some practicing on his own too, driving the rigs around the family farm. One fine day he got to experience the real thing—under the table.

"We had three loads of cattle to deliver to Burns Meat processing plant in Kitchener and neither of Dad's other drivers could do the run. So Dad drove one truck, Amsey drove the other, and I drove the third. We would have probably been fined if I'd been stopped, but sometimes things like that were necessary."

Driving a big rig would be just fine and dandy, thought this farm teen. And no exams to study for either!

8

To Baptize or Not to Baptize

In the lives of most Mennonite youngsters, church continued to play an important part right through their teens. Paul was no different. "Aside from social events, usually involving relatives, church was where you met your friends." But in one way, Paul Frey stood out from his teenage buddies. Approaching seventeen, he'd not been baptized.

Mennonites were Anabaptists, that is, they didn't baptize infants and young children, believing that the rite needed to be a conscious and mature decision. And so, Mennonite youth usually joined the church around age twelve or thirteen. Paul didn't. "I never felt called to do that," he admits. He uses "shyness" as his excuse. This "shyness" didn't sit positively with his parents, especially his mother, and he endured regular prodding about his duty.

Lucinda Frey's urgings grew in intensity as her son moved through his mid-teenage years. They reached their peak when the congregation looked forward to the annual revival rituals. Visiting speakers, including American evangelists and deacons, were brought into the various congregations to whip up religious fervor.

Preaching "fire and brimstone," to use Paul's expression, the visiting speakers would encourage the unconverted to throw off their sins, come to the front of the congregation, be welcomed warmly into the faith, and ultimately be saved. Routinely Paul remained seated while others heard the call. Eventually Mother had had enough.

"So when I was about seventeen and still not baptized, she decided to try another tactic. One day at work, I was paid a visit by our minister. I was asked if I didn't feel it was the time to be baptized like all my friends had done five or so years before. It wasn't what I'd call high pressure, but I guess I was pretty well put on the spot."

Having no great philosophical argument with the church, just what he calls "higher priorities, like hockey and baseball," Paul Frey finally took the plunge and was welcomed officially into the Mennonite Church. "It really didn't change anything for me," he acknowledges, "just that I didn't have Mom on my back!"

Admitting that at this time of his life his identity as a Mennonite was less a factor in his life than his identification with sports and his work, the adult Paul Frey is still aware of the role that the Mennonite religion played in his youthful life.

"As a young person, I was probably influenced in a number of ways without really being aware of it. Like pacifism—which is a key concept in the Mennonite philosophy. Growing up in the 1950's so soon after World War II, it made a bigger impact on me than it would have had I been born later."

Honesty and hard work also played an integral part in Paul Frey's teenage value system. They were cornerstones that would bolster him through his chosen life as an entertainer. Still, he admits that there were aspects of being Mennonite that didn't sit well with him as a teenager. The conservative women's dress was one of them. "My mother continued to wear the Mennonite cape dress and the head covering. It didn't bother me around home and around our community, but if we went into Kitchener-Waterloo, I was embarrassed."

Nor as he passed through the teenage years was he attracted to girls who dressed in the Mennonite fashion. "I looked to date girls who were modern and didn't stand out," he admits.

So too was John and Lucinda Frey's first language a source of occasional embarrassment. "Pennsylvania Dutch was my parents' common speech and it's what we spoke at home. But that embarrassed me when we were out of the Mennonite community, out in the world."

Other "out in the world" issues would challenge Paul Frey in the years ahead.

9

The Arrangement

THE ARRANGEMENT BETWEEN PAUL and his father regarding his place in the trucking business was clear-cut from the time he'd left school. Before turning sixteen, he'd work as a driver assistant in the passenger seat or at the back. After he was of legal age, he'd take his place as a full-time driver for John H. Frey.

And his salary for work done? $0. No pay. Paul explains the bargain that existed between himself and his father.[15] "Dad told me: 'You stay home and work for me and I'll make it worth your while.' And he did. Until I turned twenty-one, Dad gave me nothing for my work. Instead, he paid for whatever I wanted or needed—clothes, hockey equipment, food at a restaurant, money for dates."

Far from feeling controlled, Paul was happy about the arrangement. "Yes, I guess you could say that this part of my life was pre-planned. But I was fine with that. I never wanted for anything." The bargain would change once Paul turned twenty-one. Then John would turn over 80 percent of Frey Transport to his second son. Young Paul Frey would take over a thriving business without ever having to take out a bank loan.

Paul clearly recalls the day he took his driver's test on his sixteenth birthday. A family friend, Ken Stevens, was also a license inspector. "So I arranged to take my driver's license test with him in Kitchener. I wasn't nervous, as Ken had given me some pointers when he'd come out to the farm to visit. I drove around the block and had my license."

For this young buck, turning sixteen and being able to legally drive had another bonus. Thanks to his bargain with Dad, he took possession of his own car—a brand new Plymouth. "It was my car to drive but Dad owned it and paid all the expenses."

His pride in a flashy vehicle was genetic. Once the Frey family had changed churches and John had bought his first car, thirty years before, he remained a fervent fan of the automobile. "They were always new cars—a bit flashy, a bit of a status symbol. Dad even once bought a Lincoln."

More thrills were to come when Paul took his place, legally, behind a Frey truck. He recalls his first long solo drive. "I was delivering a load of corn from Chatham to Waterloo—a good three-hour drive on the highway. Just me, and the open road, and a ten-ton truck. Oh, that was sweet! I was as happy as I could be."

But there was more to young Paul Frey than vehicles. Clothes, girls, and hockey also ranked high on his list of likes. "I considered myself as coming from a lower-class farming family and I wanted to rise from that. So I'll confess that I liked to buy clothes. I wanted to look sharp and for other people to think that too. It was a bit of a competition with other guys."

A natural progression from a snappy wardrobe and car ownership was dating. And while the majority of the girls Paul stepped out with belonged to St. Jacobs Mennonite Church (or from the extended membership), he would, on occasion, date non-Mennonite girls.

Growing up in the hockey-mad Elmira/St. Jacobs area, Paul loved hockey too. A member of a church league team, he calls himself "a mediocre player, not a good skater." Still, he stuck with the game, as much for social reasons as any illusions of athletic grandeur. After games, the team would hang out at the Edgewood Restaurant in Elmira. Hockey gave working guy Paul Frey a chance to keep in touch with friends from school, as well as from church.

He'd continue mixing hockey with socializing with work until he was approaching his twenty-first birthday. Then the universe shifted.

Part 3

Making Room for Music

(1961–1969)

10

The Glad Tidings Quartet

"In my early years, music played only a background part of my life," says Paul. And that music was religious—church music. But what music those Mennonite churchgoers could make! In a 1986 interview with Kristina Marie Guiguet of *Music Magazine*, Paul fondly recalled: "There was no sweeter sound than four-part harmony, coming from a Mennonite congregation."[16]

"Of course it was all *a capella*," Paul explains. "Women and girls were seated on one side, and men and boys were on the other. The chorister leading the congregation stood at the front with a pitch pipe getting us in the right key." Naturally, four-part harmony was the result, with the women's soprano and alto voices blending harmonically with men's and boys' tenor and bass. In Paul's youth, Abner Martin, who went on to found the Menno Singers and the Mennonite Mass Choir in Waterloo Region, led the congregation as chorister.

As Paul's teenage buddies' voices changed, they lowered naturally to the bass and baritone tones. Paul's voice was different. "I found I couldn't get down to the lower notes that most teenage males develop. I doubt if I even knew the words of the different pitches then. But I was aware that my voice was different than most of my same age friends. And it embarrassed me."

Paul tried various strategies to change nature. "If I was standing beside someone who had a bass voice, I'd try to copy him." But to his chagrin, mimicking didn't work. But what he *could* do was reach the higher-register notes. Little could the teenage Paul Frey have foretold in these early years that his ringing tenor notes would become his fame and fortune.

Part 3: Making Room for Music

The late-1950s music scene in the Elmira/St. Jacobs area had taken on a new chapter with the formation of the Glad Tidings Quartet. Made up originally of Ray and Winston Martin, Cal Cressman and Wilf Brubacher,[17] and harmonizing a repertoire that was largely religious, gospel and spiritual, the group soon were booked solidly for weddings, anniversaries, funerals, and various other social get-togethers. Tunes such as "I Believe," "Peace in the Valley," and "I'm Bound for the Kingdom" were crowd favorites.

With music, up until this point, only in the background of Paul Frey's life—well behind trucks, hockey, and girls—he surprised himself with his interest in the Glad Tidings Quartet. The music that the group made, even more the reception that they received at events where they performed, intrigued him. Applause was, as it remained throughout his performing life, an aphrodisiac.

"'I could do that,'" I said to myself. 'I could perform in public! I just need to find a couple of guys who will sing with me.'" Taking wishing a step further, Paul formed a group (the name escapes him today) and advertised to friends and relations that they were in business. The group's first gig was at Paul's sister Lena's wedding. He recalls his emotions during this, his initial singing performance. "I was so nervous that I kept my eyes down. I was afraid that if I looked up at the audience I'd never make it through the song!" A few other bookings followed but, to Paul's disappointment, the venture fizzled.

He had little time to lament. Those reigning stars on the Woolwich County evangelical scene, the Glad Tidings Quartet, had taken note of Paul's strong tenor voice and were calling. The group had been invited to perform at a wedding in Manitoba and its current tenor, Wilf Brubacher, was unable to make the gig.

Paul Frey, age nineteen, was asked to step in as first tenor. "I said yes right away. It was an all-expenses-paid trip and I was thrilled to be asked." It would be Paul's first venture out of Ontario and he was raring to go. The experience in Manitoba only whetted his appetite to hear more applause and he admits to being wholly starstruck. With the stars clearly aligned in Paul's direction, shortly after the group's return, Paul took a call. "The Glad Tidings wanted me to join the group permanently. Wilf was leaving." Would he? Would he!

Over the next ten years, Paul's Tuesday evenings would be devoted to Glad Tidings practice. Many of his weekends were now booked with invitations to perform at church services, special religious events, weddings, anniversaries, and other celebratory events. And Paul loved it. "By now I had no trouble standing up in front an audience." Over and above the music, he loved the praise that came with signing publically. "I guess you could say I liked being popular; I liked standing out from the crowd."

And stand out he did, with his unschooled but strong tenor voice. "I could go high—even very high." But there was much vocally he couldn't do. "On a Glad Tidings recording I can hear me dropping the high notes. It's because I didn't have the breath support at that stage."

That would come in good time—and more.

11

The Schneider Male Chorus

THE GLAD TIDINGS EXPERIENCE had only whetted Paul's appetite for more music in his life. So when a friend joined the Schneider Male Chorus, a Waterloo County–based amateur vocal ensemble, and suggested that Paul may wish to audition too, he was fully receptive to the idea.

Sponsored by the processing and meat-packing company J. M. Schneider, and led by the well-respected conductor Paul Berg, the Schneider Male Chorus had been the prestige choral group in the Kitchener-Waterloo and Guelph area for decades.

A fixture on the local music scene since 1938, the Schneider Male Chorus traced its birth to a summer picnic for employees put on by J. M. Schneider Ltd. On that auspicious day, a group of the company's vocally-blessed workers had entertained with a number of selections. The response had been so positive that the singers decided that something so good needed to stick around for a while.

And so in 1939, just as World War II was declared, the Schneider Male Chorus was born. Norman C. Schneider, president and owner of the Courtland Street, Kitchener plant agreed to sponsor the singers. It was tonic for a community whose sons were heading off to war. In demand across the twin cities of Kitchener-Waterloo from its inception, the chorus initially turned its talents to raising money for the war effort.

By 1947, membership in the chorus was no longer restricted to those employed at J. M. Schneider. And at this pivotal time in its history, Paul Berg came aboard as conductor.[18] *By 1960, the Schneider Male Chorus was*

The Schneider Male Chorus

performing eight to ten concerts a year locally, and in demand both inside and outside the Kitchener-Waterloo area. Invitations to sing were coming from as far away as western venues in Canada and into the United States.[19]

Paul Frey's call to conductor Paul Berg resulted in an audition. One can only imagine Berg's reaction upon hearing the untrained voice of a young man who would, one day, become one of the world's premier operatic tenors.

"Paul Berg told me that I had a very good tenor voice but to develop it I should take voice lessons. With voice training, he predicted that I could probably eventually sing solos with the chorus," remembers Paul. The memory of this early musical prediction brings a smile to his face.

It was a delighted Paul Frey who left his audition. He'd snared a spot in the Schneider Male Chorus. And he'd think seriously about Berg's advice to look for a voice teacher. Unexpectedly, an event lurking just around the corner would give Paul increased incentive to get the task done sooner than later.

Approaching his official step into adulthood (he would turn twenty-one on April 20, 1962), Paul Frey was a busy and productive young man. The trucking business was going great guns. He had ambitions to grow it from its present three trucks to a fleet of ten. And then there were the gigs with the Glad Tidings Quartet and the Schneider Chorus.

Sports was a force in his life too: softball in the summer and hockey in the winter. Both were an opportunity to blow off steam. League hockey was a passion, although he admitted to being only a "so-so skater." During one game, the unexpected came calling. Checked hard into the boards, Paul knew immediately that his hip was dislocated. While surgery wouldn't be necessary, rehabilitation and rest would be. "I needed to take a week off work, to rest and do nothing until the injury healed." He was desolate—and more.

"I was furious—at myself. Hockey was just a hobby, nothing more, and because of it I was now laid up. Here I was about to take on full ownership of a business, and I couldn't work. Dad had to fill in for me until I was on my feet again."

In a decision that Paul calls "immediate" and "definite," he decided, on the spot, to give up hockey. "I sold my equipment right away. It was an easy choice to make. My commitment to Dad and the business was much more important than playing a game—even one I loved."

But there was an idea percolating in the back of Paul Frey's busy brain that would fill the gap left by hockey. "While I was laid up, someone had given me the album of the great singer Mario Lanza in *The Student Prince*. I was overwhelmed with Lanza's voice and the beauty of the music. 'Now that's what I need to be doing instead of ruining my body playing sports,' I told myself."

He'd follow Paul Berg's advice and find a vocal coach. As soon as he was up and around, Paul made plans to begin his training. And he could hardly wait.

12

Coming of Age

APRIL 20, 1962 SAW Paul Frey coming of age. He'd been an employee of John H. Frey since age fifteen and had proven his capabilities. Now ownership of the business (or at least 80 percent of it) came to him. It was renamed Frey Transport Ltd.

Paul had a little present for himself to celebrate the milestone. "I bought myself a Mercury convertible. It was $3,400, dark burgundy with a white top and chrome fender skirts. And it was a beauty." He disavows the misconception that to be a Mennonite means all plainness and unworldliness. "The car was a status symbol, for sure, and it made me feel successful. But I'd worked hard for that success."

He disavows the notion that Mennonites are not "status conscious." "Even the Old Orders, still driving a horse and buggy, can be successful and want to show it. They show off the handsome groomed horses and shining buggy that drives them to town, or maybe the way a Mennonite's black hat is brushed and sits on a head at a certain angle." No, Paul Frey makes clear, Mennonites and materialism can, and sometimes do, go hand in hand.

Paul had big plans for success in his newly acquired business. He'd work towards expanding the number of trucks in the Frey Transport stable. From three to ten trucks seemed doable. That would mean more employees too, up from the present three. Yes, life was good and would surely get even better.

And when he wasn't in the truck yard or on the open road, Paul was singing. He'd begun taking voice lessons with Kitchener teacher, Douglas

Campbell. In his sixties when Paul Frey came to call, Campbell had studied voice in New York. He was presently organist and choir master at St. John's Lutheran Church in Waterloo as well as teaching piano and giving singing lessons.

Paul could feel his voice growing and refining under Douglas Campbell's careful guidance. One of Campbell's first lessons was "breath support." Paul explains: "Especially when singing classical music, you need to have good breath support to allow you to hold the notes longer and stronger. The stomach is full of air like a drum and you need to be able to move it up and over your vocal chords—to hang on to the sound." Campbell's early training would stand Paul in good stead as he grew vocally over the coming years.

Paul had also found a vocal role model. He was Jon Vickers, a Saskatchewan farm boy who had burst onto the opera scene like a hard prairie wind. Vickers, built like a western bull with a personality to match, was a vocal powerhouse. He'd gotten his start in Canada just as Paul Frey's eyes and ears were opening to opera. By 1960, Vickers was wowing audiences at the Metropolitan Opera in New York, as well as the first-rung opera houses across Europe.

And while Vickers's clarion-voiced tenor mesmerized the youthful Paul Frey, he also gave inspiration for the heights to which a farm boy could aspire. "Our beginnings were so similar," comments Paul, "both coming from religious farm families."

Astutely aware of Paul's potential, Douglas Campbell began preparing him to enter vocal competitions around southwestern Ontario. In 1960's-era Ontario, that meant the annual Kiwanis Festival. Here, talented young musicians competed for honors and prestige in piano, violin, and voice.

Paul's initial jump into musical competition was in 1966 at the Toronto Kiwanis Music Festival Association. Entered into the "Amateur Male Tenor Concert Songs" category, he scored a third-place showing. The competitive twenty-five-year-old was, no doubt, disappointed, and vowed to do better. He didn't have long to wait.

Over the next two years at Kiwanis and other music festivals in Stratford, Kitchener-Waterloo, and as far east as Toronto, Paul Frey's voice and confidence only soared. Scoring marks in the high eighties to low nineties, he garnered superlatives from the judges.

"A beautiful voice—a pleasant easy tenor to listen to."

"You can't help singing with feeling."

"You command a fine line of phrase."

"Bravo. A fine voice. A real tenor with an easy resonance of production."

Paul's first press clipping, "Young St. Jacobs Tenor Festival Star on Wednesday," written in 1966 by *Kitchener-Waterloo Record* writer Michael T. Pratt, hints at the accolades to come. "It was Paul Frey night at the Kiwanis Music Festival in St. John's Church auditorium Wednesday. This young man who hails from St. Jacobs left his audience and adjudicator breathless with the quality and technique he combined in his magnificent tenor voice."[20]

Campbell's plan for his star student's musical enrichment also saw Paul branching out into amateur musical theater. His first foray was as part of the cast for the Twin City Operatic Society's 1967 production of *The King and I*. With each experience Paul was gaining confidence in both his voice and in his delivery. And with each round of applause his confidence—and his desire—grew. "I can remember thinking: 'People sing and get paid for it? That would be great! What could be more rewarding than hearing people clap for what you've done?'"

Now, featured as a soloist with the Schneider Male Chorus, Paul's star was rapidly rising. Private bookings to sing at weddings, anniversaries, and funerals also kept his weekends busy.

And to round out a well-balanced life, in 1968 Paul married Linda Horst. Linda, a registered nurse from St. Jacobs, had taken her Bachelor of Science through the University of Western Ontario and was presently a nursing instructor at St. Mary's Hospital in Kitchener. Up until his wedding, Paul had remained under his parents' roof, first at the farm, then when the elder Freys retired and moved into St. Jacobs. "I'd never considered taking a place of my own until I got married," states Paul. "There was really no reason to. I got along with my parents fine."

After their marriage, the couple moved into one of the Frey family farms between St. Clements and Heidelberg.

13

At a Musical Crossroads

BY THE CLOSING YEARS of the decade, Paul Frey was at a crossroads. Having grown markedly in voice and in performance under vocal teacher Douglas Campbell, he was being prodded by Schneider Male Chorus conductor Paul Berg to move forward in his voice coaching. Berg had named him principal soloist of the Choir and knew that with more work, with the correct coach, Paul could go far in the music world.

In an interview with the *Kitchener-Waterloo Record* of March 1970, Berg lauded his star tenor as "one of the finest voices we have ever had on our roster . . . Even at his present stage I feel he has more potential than some tenors who are already in the professional field."[21]

Berg was of the opinion that well-respected Toronto vocal coach George Lambert was the man to move Paul along. Lambert, born and raised in England, had taken his musical training in Italy and performed in the opera *La Traviata* in Rome. After a return to England for a time, he relocated to Toronto, where he appeared with Canadian symphony orchestras and opera companies. After his retirement from the stage, Lambert devoted his life to teaching. Working through the Toronto Conservatory of Music, he had coached such popular singers as Joan Maxwell and Robert Goulet, as well as operatic tenor Jon Vickers.

Now, Paul Frey found himself caught between two worlds—his bread-and-butter trucking business and the music he loved to make. Then there were the frequent comments of praise from well-meaning but uninformed admirers.

"Everybody kept saying to me: 'Why don't you become a professional singer? You're good enough for that.' I felt that too, but how was I to become a professional singer when I ran a business? I knew that I couldn't sacrifice my job for a singing career. After all, I was a married man now and we hoped to have a family one day. It did cause stress from time to time."

Eventually worn down, Paul gave in to Berg's suggestion and made an appointment to perform in Toronto for the great George Lambert. "I was curious just to see what he thought," Paul explains.

The audition went well—indeed, very well. Paul recalls: "Lambert seemed to be impressed and immediately he wanted to take me on as a student. He said: 'I could make something of you. But we'd have to work together at least two times a week.' I was honored by this but told him I would need to think about it."

In his other ear, he was hearing the practical voice of his present vocal coach, Douglas Campbell. "Douglas was a down-to-earth teacher, not given to putting what he thought were unrealistic ideas in my head. 'You are doing well as it is,' he'd remind me. 'You've got a successful business that's bringing in a comfortable income, and you're getting lots of offers to sing on the side.'" He also weighed Campbell's advisement that "the professional life is a very tough one with lots of disappointment and frustration."

It was in this state of mind that Paul returned home from the big city to the country. He knew the answer he'd give Lambert even before he opened his front door: "As much as I would have benefitted from taking classes from George Lambert, given my situation, there was no way that I could. It was impossible to leave my business to drive from St. Jacobs to Toronto twice a week." He then chastised himself: "How could I even be considering something as ridiculous as becoming a professional singer?"

And so, it was with considerable regret that the next day Paul Frey telephoned George Lambert with his answer. It was: "Thanks, I wish I could, but right now it's no." Paul had little time to regret his decision. He had to deliver a large load of hogs to Burns Meats in Kitchener the next day. Behind the wheel of his truck, taking care of business, more than once Paul muttered to himself: "I wished somebody would come up to me and say: 'Here's $10,000. Go and find out if you can make it professionally. And if that doesn't work, there'll be a guaranteed job waiting for you afterward.'"

He was leery too of accepting uninformed comments as to his "God-given gift." "A gift? I'm not sure I'd call it that. Maybe a 'God-given talent' would be closer to the way I felt. But I didn't feel that it was a God-given talent that I *must* use. I knew that there were other people who had as much talent or more than me."

Part 3: Making Room for Music

Life wasn't simple these days for Paul Frey. And it was about to get even more complicated.

Part 4

Music, Then Everything Else

(1969–1972)

14

A Musical Star Comes to Town

IN THE WINTER OF 1969, word had passed through the Kitchener-Waterloo musical grapevine that a veritable star was arriving in town. Victor Martens would be joining the Faculty of Music at Waterloo Lutheran University (now Wilfrid Laurier University, popularly known as WLU).

Martens, thirty-seven, a native of British Columbia, had graduated from "Lutheran" in 1963 and had completed four years of graduate study at the well-respected *Nordwestdeutsche Musikakademie* in Detmold, Germany. There, Martens had studied under German composer Kurt Thomas, as well as the renowned Professor Theo Lindenbaum.

An accomplished tenor, Martens would take the position of associate professor at WLU. He'd be teaching voice to students registered in the faculty. But the buzz among the community was that Martens would also be giving private lessons to students outside the faculty, including members of the public. A number of musical hopefuls had signed up before Martens even arrived in Waterloo. Paul Frey was not one of them—at least not yet. He explains his thoughts: "Men and women who were serious about improving their singing voice signed up quickly for private lessons with Victor. I didn't right away because of my loyalty to Douglas Campbell." Paul Berg reminded his Schneider Male Chorus star that opportunities like Victor Martens didn't come along every day. And so eventually Paul Frey— guilty but pragmatic—joined the line at Martens's studio door.

"I had been a student of Douglas Campbell for over five years, and he had taken me from knowing nothing to where I was now. Still, I felt that I had learned pretty well all that I could from Douglas as a teacher. I was very appreciative of what he had done for me but it was time to move on." Paul left his mentor on good terms. "He was sorry to lose me and I would miss him, but I knew that I was doing the best thing for me."

Despite Paul's earlier self-flagellation for contemplating a career as a singer after the George Lambert audition, his shift to Victor Martens gives insight into a divided heart. "Yes, I was more serious perhaps than I let on to others. I *did* want to be a professional singer and I was moving slowly to making that happen—maybe even before I really knew it."

Martens's lessons, taught in his studio/garage, were unique in form. For Paul, working full-time on the trucks, the timetable was inconvenient—and would take some maneuvering to manage. "With most music teachers, voice lessons would be once a week, usually for one hour in duration. With Victor, you went in for fifteen minutes, three to four times a week. One lesson might be just a strong vocal exercise and you were done."

The voice that came out of student Paul Frey was exceptional, whether Victor Martens heard it once a week or three to four times. Like George Lambert and Paul Berg, he was impressed with a still undeveloped talent.

Paul continued to juggle work with his private lessons over the winter of 1970–1971. He'd left the Glad Tidings Quartet after ten years of singing in the group, but remained with the Schneider Male Chorus. He took other opportunities when they came up too. And when he did, the regular dosing of "You really should be a professional singer" continued to come from well-meaning but uniformed listeners. Paul knew what it would take to follow that road. His trip to Toronto and George Lambert had told him that.

But a real opportunity to test those waters was presented to him in spring of 1971. Martens would be heading up the second year of the Summer Music Workshop to be held at Waterloo Lutheran University over four summer weeks. Martens was encouraging his private music students to enroll. Serious singers from across Canada and even the United States would be there too.

It would take some work shifting, but Paul had no intention of letting this golden opportunity pass him by.

15

The Summer Music Workshop

A PRESS RELEASE OF May 31, 1971 from the Faculty of Music at Waterloo Lutheran University had made Victor Martens's announcement official. "40 singers from Canada and the U.S., many hoping for operatic careers, will be taking part in the Canadian Summer Vocal Institute's session beginning on July 19 at Waterloo Lutheran University."[22]

The director of the session would be Martens himself. Newly appointed conductor of the Kitchener-Waterloo Symphony Raffi Armenian would also lend his expertise to the four-week program. There would be some high-powered European talent too. Dr. Theo Lindenbaum of the *Nordwestdeutsche Musikakademie* in Detmold, Germany would also be providing instruction. He'd be assisted by graduates of the Detmold school: bass Russell Smith and baritone David Falk. The news release went on to trumpet that the school was the only one of its kind in Canada.

Under the direction of these luminaries, a number of public recitals featuring students from the summer program would be offered. The group would also be mounting a concert for the community at the end of the session.

There was no doubt in Paul's mind that he would be enrolling. It was an opportunity of a lifetime for an opera novice such as himself. Fortunately, summer weather would allow him to accommodate work and music. "We usually started work at 5 a.m. to get the livestock loaded into the trucks before it got too hot. So actually I'd be through by lunch time and could attend the afternoon sessions of the summer program."

Eager to begin, Paul admits also to a feeling of intimidation at this step. "I was always intimidated when I was out there in the world. Intimidated by my lack of education, intimidated by my farm background, intimidated that I couldn't read music, intimidated that people knew more than I did."

He was fully aware that he would be the "odd man out" in such a setting. The Summer Music Workshop would certainly draw students from a variety of backgrounds and abilities: some presently enrolled full-time in WLU's Faculty of Music, some studying music at other post-secondary institutes, some with less musical training but still with a good working knowledge of the rudiments of music.

And then there was Paul—with a voice that showed great promise to come, with a burning drive to succeed and a sincere love of the operatic form, but with no formal training. This Summer Music Workshop freshman could neither read musical notes nor count beats to the bar. Few would have shown the gumption to willingly enroll in a program where they were so out of place.

When, that summer, the "green but keen" Paul met soprano Elizabeth Straus, who had attended the program the previous summer and who was back at WLU only to polish her skills, and perform for the current students, he must have felt the chasm deepen.

Elizabeth, in her early twenties, had studied voice since childhood. She'd attended the 1970 WLU Summer Music Workshop to help her determine whether teaching or performing was in her crystal ball. When Theo Lindenbaum had heard her voice, he made no secret of his opinion. Elizabeth recalls the events of that summer.[23]

"Lindenbaum decided during that summer course, after hearing me perform in a student concert, that I should come to Germany to pursue further studies and a professional career." Given that it was known that Lindenbaum had a five-year waiting list for European and Japanese students queuing at his door for lessons, the invitation came as a shock to the young Canadian.

Still, such a "gift horse" was not one Elizabeth felt she should pass over, and she accepted the esteemed professor of music's offer. She and her husband sold their car to cover the costs for her first year of study and made plans to rent their recently purchased Waterloo house. Over that year, they lived in Germany while Elizabeth studied at the *Nordwestdeutsche Musikakademie*. She then returned to Waterloo in the summer of 1971 while her mentor taught at WLU's Summer Music Workshop.

Elizabeth recalls the skills that the Summer Music Workshop students were required to master over the duration of the WLU program. "It was an expectation that we learn our arias in Italian, French, German, Russian, Spanish, Tagalog, Hebrew, or English, whatever the original language for the score was." She calls language acquisition "one of the tools of the profession." As such, facility in foreign languages would be "the test which separated the sincere artists from the casual singers."

Most students enrolled in the program would have background in at least one foreign language—French, others French and Italian. And then there was Paul Frey. "I spoke English and Pennsylvania German." Neither would be of much help to him learning opera librettos. His French, reluctantly studied over fifteen years ago in grade nine, was long lost. He'd surely have his work cut out for himself.

With time limited, the group would immediately begin preparing for their recital. It would be performed for the general public at the conclusion of the four-week session. Entitled "Scenes from Opera," the gala would feature five excerpts from well-known operas: *Faust, Die Fledermaus, Albert Herring, Der Freischütz,* and *Die Zauberflöte*. Each of the forty-five students enrolled would have an opportunity to take a role.

No doubt in recognition of his promising voice, Paul Frey grabbed the role of Faust in the four-character *Faust* presentation. He had never heard, nor been aware of, the work. Almost fifty years later, Paul recalls his emotions as he heard French composer Gounod's score for the first time. "I was truly overwhelmed by the beauty and the wonder of it—and that I was going to be given the chance to sing it."

"Overwhelming" might be the most apt description of the task before him too in learning the part. *Faust's* libretto was in French. Paul's working vocabulary of the language barely went past *bonjour* and *au revoir*. But if academics were lacking, initiative was not. He recalls the regimen he followed to prepare himself for his first operatic performance.

"The first thing I did was buy a recording of *Faust* to get an idea of how it goes. And I played it over and over and over again." The second step was infinitely more arduous than soaking in the beauty of the French language. "I bought a French-English dictionary and began to translate the words—most of which I had no idea what they meant."

And while he could book some time with a Summer Music Workshop coach to help him along the way, for the most part, Paul was on his own. Despite the monumental challenges this young man faced, he calls his introduction to opera "exciting." "I had a duet with a soprano and also a very nice aria with a high C in it. And I could hit it easily." No doubt, despite his obvious lack of schooling, a shining talent was duly noted by the professional musicians in attendance. "High Cs are generally considered the highest note a tenor has to hit and not all even the professionals can reach it," explains Paul.

Despite his outstanding vocal abilities, Paul denies being exceptional within the group. "If I did stand out in any way, it was probably because I didn't know what I was doing." But he knew a star when he saw one and that was surely the beautiful Elizabeth Straus. "When Elizabeth was there, in the room and singing, you got the feeling that you were in the presence of someone very special."

And so Paul Frey and the other students in 1971's Summer Music Workshop (including Paul's younger brother Ken) burned the midnight oil in the rehearsal hall, putting the final touches on their public performance. In his review of "Scenes from Opera," *Kitchener-Waterloo Record* music writer W. J. Pitcher reported that "the audience was treated to many highlights of outstanding vocalism and artistry."[24] Pitcher also noted in his review that the esteemed Professor Lindenbaum was quoted as observing that "five or six of the class show real potential for professional careers."

Paul Frey hoped that one of them was himself.

Paul is uncertain when, over that first golden summer, the penny had dropped. It may have come during the first moments of hearing *Faust*. "I had never heard music like that before and I totally fell in love with it." It may have come as he struggled through learning his solo part. It had been devilishly hard to get it right, but work, perseverance, and an iron will had brought rewards. It was certainly before the curtain closed on "Scenes from Opera" and hearing the applause for his strong performance. But drop the penny did—with a resounding "ping."

"I'd decided that I wanted to pursue opera full-time. I wanted to be a professional opera singer. I didn't know how I was going to go about it and I wasn't sure how this was going to work out with my truck company, but I knew that it was something I had to do."

On more than one occasion, Paul and his wife, Linda, had talked about his passion to sing and how this might affect their life as they knew it presently. And while the way to achieving his dream was presently clouded, Paul felt that Theo Lindenbaum—and Germany—held the key. He would speak to his professor. He was going to ask the great man to take him on as a full-time student in Germany.

Paul admits to a feeling of insecurity over his musical abilities as he mentally rehearsed how and when he would make the approach. "What if he said no? What then?" Taking advantage of a solo coaching session with Lindenbaum, Paul Frey popped the question. "I asked him if I could study at Detmold with him." Surprisingly, and without hesitation, Lindenbaum answered "yes."

With the question asked and response given, the two worked out a plan. "He suggested that I continue my training in Canada over the coming year. And as he was committed to coming back to Waterloo for a follow-up Summer Music Workshop in 1972, I would follow him back to Germany and begin my lessons in the fall."

Paul Frey floated through the rest of the afternoon as if in a dream. Now to put the pieces of the puzzle together. Selling the trucking business came first.

16

Putting the Puzzle Together

THE INTERVIEW THAT PAUL gave *Kitchener-Waterloo Record* music columnist W. J. Pitcher in the summer of 1972 only hints at the excitement he felt in putting together the pieces of his plan to study music full-time. "Professor Theodore Lindenbaum of Germany readily encouraged me to give it a try and accepted me as a pupil in his class at the Detmold Academy for next September," he fairly bubbled to the reporter.[25]

Not all friends and family shared Paul's exuberance: "Linda wasn't opposed to the plan, but I know the whole idea was scary to her," Paul recalls. "My father was disappointed that the truck company he'd built and passed on to me was going to go. My mother just thought I was making a terrible mistake. She was also worried about me living in what she thought was 'too worldly' a life. And my circle of friends? I guess surprise is the best way to describe their reaction. They probably all thought I was crazy, but just didn't say."

Depending on the day, or the commentator and the comment heard, Paul readily admits to having his doubts too about the step he was taking. "I'd tell myself that going off to study music wasn't a very responsible thing to do for a married man who hoped to have children. It was when I was thinking that way that I'd listen to people who suggested I just find somebody to run the business for a couple of years till I could sort things out. But then I'd have a change of heart and tell myself that this was something I had to do. It was all or nothing. I'd give it five years and if it didn't work I could start again. I'd still be young."

Five years. Now that made some sense!

Putting the Puzzle Together

Paul's initial step enacting his plan was to put the word out to the agricultural community that Frey Transport was for sale. It didn't take too long for an offer to come in. It was from Mardale Transport in Floradale. Along with the bid came a couple of conditions: the first was that Paul would continue to work for the company for six months as the transition took place. A second stipulation was that if he returned to Canada within five years of leaving for Germany, he wouldn't start a new trucking company. "Insurance that I wouldn't try to take old customers back," he explains.

By the end of 1971, Paul Frey was unemployed. Mardale Transport now owned Frey Transport. Paul could now use his newfound freedom and money in the bank to continue preparing for studies with Theo Lindenbaum. He left no stone unturned in his tutoring. Private voice lessons with Victor Martens continued. Martens, a fervent Lindenbaum disciple, was overjoyed at Paul's decision and predicted only success.

Still unable to read music, Paul also signed on for private piano lessons with Howard Dyck, who was leading the Kitchener-Waterloo Philharmonic Choir and teaching at WLU part-time. "Remember, I didn't know a middle C from an F sharp," he chuckles. "I felt that being able to at least have a basic idea of the musical scale would help me learn what I was singing." Paul mimes the Frey "two-finger approach" to musical scores.

Howard Dyck remembers the young man who'd sold his thriving business to strike out "on a flyer."[26] "He was virtually a musical illiterate when I first met him in 1972. So he learned by rote. And this made him insecure—insecure far longer than he should have." "But," Howard adds, "seldom have I met a person who wanted to learn more." Despite these considerable drawbacks, once Paul Frey got onto a stage he was a "commanding figure—with a fabulous voice."

Paul had also arranged to have coaching lessons with Raffi Armenian, the newly-appointed conductor of the Kitchener-Waterloo Symphony. From his home in Montreal, conductor Armenian recalls his working relationship, almost fifty years ago, with the determined Paul Frey.[27]

"My major memories of Paul were his immense insecurities about his musical abilities. He'd have difficulties finding the notes and he took longer than most to master them. But every so often this beautiful, wonderful sound would show itself and you could see what he was capable of."

Part 4: Music, Then Everything Else

Taking advantage of every opportunity he had to sing publically was part of Paul's plan too. One of these was at the 60th anniversary celebrations of Waterloo Lutheran University. At this gala production, three choirs and a number of soloists entertained a capacity crowd at WLU's theater auditorium. *Kitchener-Waterloo Record*'s music critic Pitcher, Paul's number one journalistic cheerleader, singles him out in the paper's review of the evening. "With good tenors a rarity, I was particularly impressed by the new vocal look of Mr. Paul Frey in his projection of [the aria] *Deposuit Potentes* from the *Bach Magnificat*."[28]

17

A Cautionary Word from a Star

PAUL'S CONNECTION TO PAUL Berg, Choral Director of the Schneider Male Chorus remained strong. To the *Kitchener-Waterloo Record* music writer Pitcher, Berg lauded his star tenor: "even at his present stage, I feel he [Frey] has more potential than some tenors who are in the professional field."[29]

With such raw talent before him, Paul Berg was endeavoring to use his connections in the music world to assist Paul Frey to reach that potential. One of these connections was with contralto Maureen Forrester, one of Canada's most renowned operatic singers. Highly respectful of Forrester's musical savvy, Berg arranged for Paul to have a private vocal session with her. He knew the forthright star would speak frankly and honestly of his abilities—and potential.

Awed by the star power of the great Forrester, to his credit, Paul still sang confidently at her home in Toronto. He recalls her comments: "They were positive and thoughtful. 'You seem to have what it takes vocally to make a career in music' she told me. 'But you have to know yourself, if you have what it takes to make it in a very tough business. You have to be sure it's really what you want.'"

Paul *was* sure and felt he had the determination and resilience to follow what might be a rocky path. He returned home cautiously optimistic. Over the winter of 1971–1972, he resigned from his position of principal soloist at the Schneider Male Chorus to concentrate on opera. But as a favor to his friend Paul Berg, he agreed to accompany the group on their June tour of western Canada. It was during this tour that Berg had a heart-to-heart with his star tenor. Paul recalls the conversation. Little could he have guessed in the months to come how crucial this would be to his present plans.

"Paul Berg questioned my decision to go to Germany, reminding me that there was an excellent Opera School at the University of Toronto, as well as some in the U.S. He felt that it wasn't necessary to disrupt my life as much as I was doing and suggested that I go for an audition for the school in Toronto. 'What have you got to lose?' he asked me."

As much to please his friend than from any other motive, Paul made the requisite arrangements and got himself to the University of Toronto audition. Quite the daunting situation for a "sight-reading illiterate." Still, Paul was relaxed as he sang before the Opera School selection committee. "I was calm. There was no pressure on me because, after all, I was headed to Germany. This trip to the Opera School was really only fulfilling the request of a friend. So as a result, I sang very well. I finished and they immediately offered me admission. I thanked them for the opportunity but deferred. I told them I was headed to Germany!"

Paul Frey could scarce have predicted how such certainty and confidence would scatter with the icy wind that waited around the corner.

As the 1972 WLU Summer Music Workshop approached, Paul's enthusiasm for the monumental step he had taken was in full bloom. Any doubts that he had harbored about the decision he was making had faded into a sense of unbridled joy for the colors of his future. He and Linda had rented out their St. Clements home and arrangements had been made to take an apartment in Detmold, Germany. They would leave soon after the conclusion of the Institute program and Paul would immediately begin his studies with Professor Lindenbaum.

The outlook for year two of the Summer Music Workshop looked exciting too. Over the four-week session, the students would be tackling the Verdi *Requiem*, with a gala performance at the conclusion. Again, Victor Martens would be in charge of the production, with assistance from K-W Symphony Orchestra conductor Raffi Armenian. Howard Dyck, now on the WLU music faculty, as well as leading the K-W Philharmonic Choir, was also lending his expertise. And of course Professor Theo Lindenbaum had made the trip from Detmold. Paul counted the hours till the first day of class.

Paul's memory of when the bottom dropped out of his dreams is uncertain. "But I think it was early in the program and it was done privately,"

A Cautionary Word from a Star

he reflects. In any case, the words coming from Professor Theo Lindenbaum's mouth were shattering. "He took me aside and told me that his health wasn't good. As a result, his doctors were advising him not to take on any new students come the fall. He was sorry but he'd have to take back his offer of teaching me privately in Germany."

"Thunderstruck" best describes Paul's state of mind at the pronouncement. Lindenbaum's next utterance did little to soften the crushing blow. "But I know I'll see you some day on the stage of the Metropolitan Opera House in New York," offered the professor with a smile. Paul walked through the rest of the day as if in a dark and troubling dream.

With email and texting only a notion in a technology wizard's brain, Paul needed to wait until he returned home to pass the bad news on to his wife, Linda. "She was shocked, for sure, but I can truthfully say she was relieved too. What we'd planned to do would have been pretty disruptive to our lives."

And if truth be told, once the weight of the rejection had passed, Paul was relieved. "I'm really not sure if I was fully prepared for the step I was about to take." Recalling the twist of fate that came with Theo Lindenbaum's dramatic words almost fifty years later, he is reflective.

"It was pretty obvious from the off-handed tone he used, that he had no idea what I'd had to do in my life to allow me to take the step to come to Germany. He had no clue the position his change of heart had put me in."

Paul also ponders how Professor Lindenbaum's health allowed him to teach in Canada for four weeks but not take on a new student in Germany. Not given to bitterness, he had no choice but to move on. Retired Faculty of Music professor at Wilfrid Laurier University and opera bass-baritone Daniel Lichti, who did study with Lindenbaum in Germany after Paul's disappointment, indicates his own luck came down to being at the right place at the right time.

"I only got into Lindenbaum's studio when I did because I happened to call him from Toronto in the same week that one of his students, from South Africa, backed out. She had been offered a contract at Vienna State Opera. Otherwise, I would have been waiting for at least a year."

Lichti adds: "I can well imagine Lindenbaum's words would have shattered Paul at the time." "Shattered" Paul Frey might have been, but this country boy was made of more formidable fiber than to give up his dream. Luckily, he had a few people in his court to help him dust himself off and continue down the road he'd started.

Part 5

Opera School: Odd Man Out

(1972–1977)

18

Picking Up the Pieces

THE SECOND PERSON TO learn the sorry details of Paul Frey's shattered dream was his friend and Schneider Male Chorus conductor, Paul Berg. Berg was ready and able to suggest a plan that might take away some of the pain. "Give the people at the University of Toronto a call right away," suggested Berg. "Remember you've been accepted into the school, so all's not lost."

Berg's words acted as a salve on Paul Frey's battered soul. "I took Berg's advice, and called the University of Toronto Opera School the next day. I told them that my plans had changed and I would not be going to Germany. I wondered if it was too late for me to accept their offer of admission for the fall."

It was *not* too late, and the University would be happy to include him on their Opera School roll for September of 1972. "I reminded them that I could barely read a note of music, but that seemed not to be significant. 'We'll teach you all that when you get here,' they told me."

Paul recalls breathing an immense sigh of relief as he accepted the offer. In the days to come, the sigh would resonate. "Where would I have been if I'd not followed Paul Berg's advice last winter? Where would I be if I hadn't applied to the Toronto Opera School and gone for the audition? No truck business, no school in Germany. What an embarrassing mess it would have been."

His path clear, Paul could now give measured thought to Lindenbaum's rejection. "I wondered if what had happened was for the best. Maybe moving to Germany was too big a step for me at that stage in my life. Relocating to Toronto was certainly going to be less disruptive to our lives." He was

Part 5: Opera School: Odd Man Out

now able to give his all to completing—and enjoying the rest of the Summer Music Workshop session.

In late August 1972, Paul and Linda Frey were off to Europe on a fact-finding holiday. "I figured that if I was going to be an opera singer, I better first see some opera," he laughs. Former WLU Summer Music Workshop student Elizabeth Straus, who'd taken up Lindenbaum's offer of lessons in Germany two years before, remained there and offered to put up the Freys during their vacation.

And while Theo Lindenbaum had remained firm in declining Paul as a full-time student, he was agreeable to him taking a few morning voice lessons after the professor returned from Canada. With no bitterness shown, Paul availed himself of the opportunity to work with the eminent Lindenbaum in this abbreviated form. "I took several fifteen-minute mini-lessons, like I'd had with Victor Martens in Waterloo," explains Paul.

In the afternoon, the Freys would be tourists, taking in the glorious sights of Europe. Evenings were reserved for attending operatic performances—in Germany and Austria. The opera buzz that surrounded the spectacular Viennese performances especially wowed this country boy. "People lined up to get opera tickets like they did to get Toronto Maple Leaf tickets at home! It was standing room only inside and if someone left their place for any reason, they might come back to find it taken."

Someday, and with any luck, he'd be part of that world.

Word had spread throughout the tight-knit Mennonite community that things hadn't worked out for Paul Frey going to Germany to sing. Instead he'd be doing something equally unexpected—that is, he'd be attending Opera School in the big city of Toronto. At least one neighbor found that circumstance to his advantage. Mr. Abner Martin, part owner of the Kitchener Stockyards and president of Holstein-Friesen Cattle Association, wondered if Paul would be interested in singing at the Cattle Association's annual convention at the Four Seasons Hotel in Toronto.

Any opportunity to sing publically interested the fledgling opera tenor and he enthusiastically agreed. There was a catch though. He'd need to audition for a talent agent first, but Martin assured Paul he'd be a shoo-in for the gig. As predicted, the agent liked what he heard and gladly took Paul on as a client. The connection would prove a valuable one in more ways than a one-night convention stand.

Picking Up the Pieces

The agent knew Dr. David Ouchterlony, organist and choir director of the Timothy Eaton United Church, one of the biggest and most prestigious churches in Toronto. It seems that the church was looking for a tenor who would sing regularly at Sunday church services. The job, which paid well, would include being a part of the church choir as well as soloist. The agent encouraged Paul to apply and to attend the audition with two pieces of music prepared. Memory of the conversation between novice tenor Paul Frey and the esteemed Dr. Ouchterlony that came out of the audition still causes Paul to smile.

"I sang the two pieces that I'd prepared. Dr. Ouchterlony accompanied me on the organ. He seemed quite impressed but then handed me an unfamiliar piece of music and asked me to sing it. I had to admit that I couldn't read sheet music, but I was working on it. It was embarrassing for sure, and I was certain that he'd show me the door."

Instead, unfazed, the director looked at the youthful applicant and replied: "Well, these days if you can find a tenor who can hold the music the right side up you're fortunate." And so, faulty sight reading or not, Paul Frey got the job as lead tenor at Timothy Eaton United Church.

He gives some background on the "dumb tenor" label. "I've heard that the label comes from the idea that tenors seem to be able to just march onto the stage and sing and blow the audience away—without much effort. So the legend grew up that, with tenors, it was just the sound that matters—there wasn't much going on behind the voice." He adds that one of the world's greatest tenors, Luciano Pavarotti, was a weak note reader. This gave substance to the "dumb tenor" legend.

Whether the larger-than-life Pavarotti suffered embarrassment due to his deficits is doubtful. Paul Frey did. "I was the lead tenor, but all the other tenors could read music." He had joined three other soloists who would sing at Sunday services: a soprano, a contralto, and a baritone. Each had committed themselves to three services a week. "We alternated and gave our solo performances about every four weeks," explains Paul.

And the salary for giving up his Sunday mornings? "I think I earned $200 each week," recalls Paul. No small loose change by early 1970's standards.

19

Back to School

PAUL AND LINDA HAD rented a house in Mississauga and Paul planned to drive into the city for classes on the sprawling University of Toronto campus. It was surely an abrupt change of scene for this country boy more used to the dust flying, bumping down country roads.

Still, he'd meet his share of bumps and bruises over the coming months at Canada's largest opera school.

The University of Toronto Opera School, founded in 1946 on a minuscule budget of $500, had grown considerably since its early days. In 1972 it offered three programs: the two-year diploma, the three-year Bachelor of Arts degree, and the Master's degree. Whereas the BA and MA programs required academic qualifications, the diploma program did not.

Courses were offered in operatic repertoire, vocal, movement (acting), languages—French, Italian and German—and in fencing. Each student would also be paired with a coach who would work closely developing voice and interpretation of music.

As he anticipated the opening of his program, Paul's emotions were mixed. "I'd been out of school since I was fourteen. I was now thirty-two. I was nervous—I always was nervous when I was 'out there' in the world. But I was eager to begin too." With no high school graduation diploma, Paul was registered in the two-year diploma program. His voice-in-bloom alone had given him admission.

He joined a class of approximately thirty students—females outnumbering males by three to one. The majority of them had studied music

Back to School

throughout secondary school; some were graduates of a university Bachelor of Music program. Paul knew from the beginning that he was, academically, the odd one out. "My lack of education was a detriment for sure. I had so much ground to catch up on."

Language training was only one area that needed considerable remedial work. Many of Paul's classmates had studied French throughout secondary school; others had taken Spanish or German. "I'd taken French in grade nine but that was seventeen years ago, and the Pennsylvania Dutch or Amish/Mennonite German we spoke at home sure wasn't the High German of opera."

Having brushed up on his scant high school French when he had agonizingly mastered his role in *Faust* for the WLU Summer Music Workshop, Paul now looked forward to more hard work in the language. This labor would continue to the end of his career. "French always remained harder for me to learn than Italian." Hard slogging, learning his "*le*" from his "*la*" from his "*les*" was the order of the day. German was, not surprisingly, easy for him to master. He'd also taken some conversational German classes over the winter when he anticipated studying in Germany.

On the other hand, days when he learned from the great baritone Louis Quilico were joyful ones. Quilico, born in Montreal in 1925, made his debut at the Metropolitan Opera in 1955 and went on to sing on the stages of Covent Garden, La Scala, and in Paris. Quilico is most renowned for his performances in Verdi's *Rigoletto*.

By 1970, Quilico and his wife, Lina, had returned to Canada and both began teaching in the Faculty of Music of the University of Toronto, particularly at the Opera School. "Louis Quilico was a wonderful teacher, but he was also a busy professional singer," recalls Paul. "And when he had performance dates, he didn't teach; Lina filled in for him. She was just as excellent."

Paul credits Quilico with developing the "ping" that would allow his unamplified operatic voice, especially singing Wagnerian opera, to carry past a large orchestra. Quilico's instruction taught his opera students to move the voice from the throat, where it naturally comes up, into the sinuses. "This," explains Paul, "gives the voice the resonance needed in a large opera house." Paul would, in time, master the heavenly "ping."

If all days could have been Louis Quilico days . . . But for Paul Frey there was the matter of his non-existent sight-reading skills. His abject weakness in this key area was observed by his Opera School vocal coach, Dr. George Brough. Paul explains his agony:

Part 5: Opera School: Odd Man Out

"We'd be given an excerpt from an opera to learn—very difficult, almost impossible for me as they were primarily in French or Italian. And of course I couldn't read music. And each day, we'd practice it with our vocal coach. Mine was Dr. Brough and I think I drove him crazy. I don't think he'd ever worked with someone who had so many deficits as me—who'd had as little musical training as me. And he got frustrated—regularly. George Brough had no patience with me."

If there was solace in company, Paul had a glimmer. In front of another piano, with another vocal coach, another first-year Toronto Opera School student was also scraping at the bottom on the sight-reading barrel. "He was an Italian student who was almost as weak as me," offers Paul. "But this guy had an advantage, as he could speak Italian."

Soon a remedial sight-reading class was set up with Paul and his Italian classmate as the most needy. They were joined by a few others also deemed in want of remediation. "It started off with about ten of us, but the numbers soon dwindled." Likening the University of Toronto Opera School "Remedial Sight Reading" to a special education class whose members would do anything to remove the stigma, Paul recalls the numbers depleting until he and his Italian colleague were the only ones remaining. "And at that, the instructor decided it wasn't worth his time to do it. So the class was discontinued."

Paul was now on his own to shore up his obvious deficiencies. He enrolled in sight-reading classes at the Royal Conservatory of Music in the city. His signature work ethic came to the fore again. With dedication and diligence, Paul slowly progressed. "But I was always behind; my instructors soon learned that it took me much longer to learn some things than most of the other students."

There were some social adjustments as well. His conservative, rural Mennonite "in this world, not of this world" background had done little to prepare him for big-city diversity. "In my class some of the males were gay. One of the instructors was openly gay. It was my first exposure to the gay community and I do admit it was a shock. I was so unprepared for the world 'out there.'"

Despite his academic weaknesses, Paul had no difficulty making social connections. His unassuming, soft-spoken, and understated ways made gaining friends easy. "There weren't too many other farmers there, but it wasn't high society either. I got along well," he recalls of these challenging years. His work ethic won him fans too.

"I took the philosophy that this was like a race. If I was going to have a chance at winning, I was just going to have to work harder than the others. And so, that's what I did; it's what I'd always done. Whether it was cleaning out a pig stable or singing an opera, I just had to do it to the very best of my abilities."

20

More Moonlighting

IN THE EVENINGS AND weekends, when he could get them, Paul took singing gigs in his home Waterloo area and further afield. He snatched a plum when Canadian contralto diva Maureen Forrester came to town in early 1973.

Forrester had agreed to perform with the Kitchener-Waterloo Symphony Orchestra, under conductor Raffi Armenian. She'd be starring in Bizet's *Carmen*. With star power well beyond the K-W Symphony Orchestra's usual guest performers, Forrester's appearance was a coup. Those who took supporting roles would be assured of wide press coverage. Thanks to Armenian, the role of Le Remendado, the smuggler, would be played by Paul Frey.

The conductor and the tenor had become acquainted at the WLU Summer Music Workshop, and Armenian had coached Paul for a period of time before Opera School. Armenian recalled in a 2019 interview: "I was pleased to hear that Paul had gotten into Opera School, and even more pleased that he was benefitting from the coaching of the great Louis Quilico." He adds: "Quilico was a better fit, as a coach, for Paul than Victor Martens had been in Waterloo."

Paul laughs, recalling the "wheeling and dealing" that went on between himself and the affable conductor over the Forrester appearance. "Raffi offered me the part of Le Remendado without an audition, but he said that he couldn't pay me. I was OK with that but I suggested that maybe he could do me a favor in return. He would serve as my accompanist at a later concert I'd be giving at Conrad Grebel College, at the University of Waterloo. And he agreed."

More Moonlighting

The Bizet night was clearly the great Forrester's, although a review by music critic John Kraglund of the *Globe and Mail* took note of Paul Frey. The tenor, observed Kraglund, portentously "gave evidence of talent in need of further experience."[30]

A month later, and on home turf again, Paul took center stage in a recital before a capacity crowd at Conrad Grebel College's annual music and lecture series. Raffi Armenian fulfilled his part of the bargain by accompanying Paul on the piano.

In his review of March 13, 1973, "Frey Development shown in Conrad Grebel debut," *Kitchener-Waterloo Record* music critic W. J. Pitcher's laudatory comments focused on the audience reaction to their "hometown boy." "If Mr. Frey's future appearances are as well-received as this one, he can continue to take an optimistic view of the career decision he made a year ago at the age of 30."[31]

One of Paul's favorite moonlighting gigs was appearing on the Bob McLean Show, an early CHCH Hamilton talk show. Hollywood's minor luminaries, such as Frank Sinatra Jr. and comedian Dom DeLuise, would occasionally share the spotlight with local folk, like opera singer Paul Frey. "It was great fun," he reminisces.

Another memorable gig saw him singing at a Masonic Temple! "They wouldn't let you go anywhere by yourself," Paul chuckles. "Someone walked you in, walked you out, and stayed with you as long as you were in the building. Secretive for sure!"

Back in the classroom, the routine for Paul was less rewarding. "Well into my first year, I still couldn't read music; I couldn't count three beats to the bar and I couldn't read or understand French. So the 'dumb tenor' label stuck. And it wasn't pleasant." Looking back on his first year at the University of Toronto's Opera School, Paul has few warm memories. The inspired presence of Louis Quilico is one.

The payoff for the long hours in the classroom and from the coaching sessions was performance—the chance to sing for audiences. The University of Toronto's Opera School gave two, sometimes three public performances during the year. For those students in their first year of the program, the playbill would be opera excerpts; in the second year, full operas would be staged. The "shining star" soprano, tenor, baritone, and bass voices would win the solo roles. Lesser lights would support the stars in the chorus.

Part 5: Opera School: Odd Man Out

Four tenors, including Paul Frey, vied for star roles in the class of 1972–1973. "The two who were the better sight readers got the choicer parts," Paul remembers, "and my Italian classmate, who couldn't sight read, and I routinely got chorus parts."

His first "bit part" solo role came in a spring 1973 performance, singing the role of the Duke of Mantua in an excerpt from Verdi's *Rigoletto*. Paul's cheerleader, *Kitchener-Waterloo Record* music writer W. J. Pitcher, was in the audience too. Pitcher calls it "one of the best-received efforts in the season-closing program of the school."[32]

It appears that Pitcher had also asked for a commentary on the local singer's performance from Canadian Opera Company Director Herman Geiger-Torel. Geiger-Torel offers modest praise: "He has a very good voice and he has done well in his first year of training here."[33] Paul wouldn't be showing off those comments to family and friends!

Students enrolled in the Opera School were also encouraged to audition to become part of the Canadian Opera Company (COC) chorus. In the mid to late 1970's, the COC worked in tandem with the Opera School. A look into the formation and growth of this cornerstone of Canadian opera is timely.

The Royal Conservatory Opera Company was founded directly following the establishment of the University of Toronto Opera School. Nicholas Goldschmidt was musical director, with Felix Brentans as stage director. Herman Geiger-Torel succeeded Brentans as stage manager in 1948.

1949 saw the company's first production of five operatic excerpts, performed at Hart House Theatre at the University of Toronto. This was followed by complete productions at Eaton's Auditorium, the Royal Alexandra Theatre, and the Art Gallery of Ontario.

The company's first opera festival in 1950 (considered the true beginning of the COC) featured Don Giovanni, Rigoletto, *and* La Bohème. *All were performed at the Royal Alexandra Theatre. At this point, the financial cooperation between the Royal Conservatory of Music and the COC ended and COC became an incorporated entity.*

Herman Geiger-Torel assumed responsibility as the company's artistic director in 1956 and Goldschmidt took the role of musical director.

More Moonlighting

Official links with the Opera School were severed the same year. The company now looked to employ professional opera singers. Still, the COC continued to offer support and cooperation to the school and used its facilities.

The company was renamed the Canadian Opera Association in 1960 and performed over a seven-week fall season. It later became officially known as the Canadian Opera Company.

Staging primarily at the O'Keefe Centre in the 1960's and 1970's (when the O'Keefe was first renamed the Hummingbird Centre, then the Sony Centre for the Performing Arts), the COC moved to its permanent home in 1998, the Four Seasons Centre for the Performing Arts.

Paul had auditioned to be part of the Canadian Opera Company and was delighted to be accepted into their numbers. "Not all made it into the company, so I was very happy." That the position offered pay was a bonus. Content to sing in the chorus at the outset, tenor Paul Frey would hope for more as his skills progressed.

Classes ended in June and students went their own way over the summer months. Paul and Linda had chosen to remain in Toronto and Paul found employment as a truck driver for Sealtest, delivering ice cream to grocery stores. Driving a big semi-trailer, the ex-trucker was a natural behind the wheel—even with the traffic congestion of downtown Toronto. The job started early and he was finished by mid-afternoon. This allowed him time for practice and appearances at the various gigs around the city and further afield. Sunday remained devoted to Timothy Eaton United Church.

The Freys were quite settled in the big city and Paul was looking for year two of Opera School to best year one. "Yes, my first year was a bit of a washout," he admits.

21

Opera School Encore

PAUL'S SECOND YEAR AT Opera School began on a much higher note than the first had ended. He'd convinced the school to pair him with a new coach—one who might not find him as much as a challenge as had Dr. Brough.

After some negotiation, Richard Fisher, an Englishman, was assigned to Paul Frey. It was a good match. "He took me under his wing; I made good progress in counting and reading notes." Paul had continued his private sight-reading tutorials at the Royal Conservatory and these, with coach Fisher's encouragement, did much to improve his battered self-confidence.

He continued growing musically too with the COC—albeit in the chorus. It was in the wings of the O'Keefe Centre, where the company staged their operas, when he first heard German composer Richard Wagner. And he was mesmerized.

The company was staging Wagner's *Der Fliegende Hollander* (*The Flying Dutchman*). "Hollander" was one of Wagner's early compositions and concerned a ship's captain who is condemned to sail the oceans until doomsday. The unfortunate sailor's only respite will come when he finds a woman who promises faithfulness to the death. Every seven years he is allowed to land to search for just such a woman.

Paul recalls the music coming from the orchestra and the opera company as *ubermenschlich* (otherworldly). So much so that he chose to forsake rest and relaxation in the "green room" with other members of the chorus when they were not needed on stage. He'd instead stand behind the stage curtain to fill his ears—and soul—with the divine sound. "At the time I felt that there was no way my voice could ever be that good—good enough to sing those arias. It seemed so far above me."

Still, he was slowly gaining a measure of self-confidence elsewhere. He'd become friends with Stan Kane, who also sang in the COC chorus. Kane had dreams of being a professional opera singer too, but, like Paul, was relegated to minor roles. But Stan was shining as a male model and he felt Paul could earn some money in front of the camera too. He pointed Paul in the direction of an agent who could get him some work.

Stan's hunch was accurate and Paul was quickly signed—no experience needed. Work came primarily for print advertisements, although Paul recalls smiling for a toothpaste commercial! A full-page advertisement for The Bay of January 22, 1975 features a mustachioed Paul Frey wearing a Bay sweater. He did a few voice ads on radio as well. "I got maybe ten jobs in all; it was fun and the money was good."

There was cause for celebration on the home front too. Paul and Linda Frey's son Benjamin was born on August 24, 1974.

When Paul was admitted to the University of Toronto Opera School, it was in the two-year diploma program. Having made enormous strides over those years, he was also aware that there was considerable more progress to be made. Under these circumstances, he was allowed to return for a third year.

Joining him that year was another Waterloo County farm boy: bass-baritone Daniel Lichti. Over the pair's time together at the University of Toronto's Opera School, Lichti gained insight into the curious case of Paul Frey. "Paul was treated terribly by the school, and, I can honestly say, he was verbally abused by at least one of the school personnel. That was bad enough. But he was continually overlooked for parts that he should have had." Lichti points to favoritism in this regard. "The people who made the decisions about who would get the main parts had their favorites. And it was clear that Paul was not one of them. And it happened time and time again."[34]

As the year progressed and other tenors snagged lead roles, Paul's frustration grew. "I continued to be passed over for the major parts, even though I had the voice to take them." Recognition would have to come from engagements outside the Opera School.

Over 1974–1975, Paul Frey's performance calendar was packed: appearances with the University of Toronto and Mississauga Symphonies, in Gilbert & Sullivan Society's production of *The Mikado* at the Hart House Theatre, at the newly opened National Arts Centre in Ottawa in *The Magic*

Flute, and back home in Kitchener-Waterloo to star in the Mennonite Mass Choir with the K-W Symphony's performance of *The Creation*.

He'd continued his Sunday gig at Timothy Eaton Church. In those heady days of growing church membership and overflowing church coffers, large and affluent churches, especially in Toronto, could afford paid soloists. At Timothy Eaton, Paul was one of four featured and was joined for Sunday services by a soprano, a bass, and a baritone soloist. Nor was the tony Eaton church alone in its hiring of Sunday singers. Paul's co-stars in a K-W performance of *The Creation*, soprano Constance Newlands and bass John Neibour, also held Sunday jobs at large Toronto churches: Newlands at Metropolitan United Church, and Neibour at St. George United Church.

As Paul's calendar filled, so did the glowing press reviews. Joining his faithful cheerleader, W. J. Pitcher of the *Kitchener-Waterloo Record*, were now big-city journalists. Herb Michaels, covering "Evening at the Opera" with the Mississauga Symphony, calls Paul Frey's presentation of Gounod's *Faust*, Saint Saens's *Samson and Delila*, and Verdi's *La Traviata* "an exceptionally good interpretation of the roles," with his "strong singing voice projecting well."[35]

The closing months of 1975 brought unfortunate news too. After a short illness, on November 14, 1975, Paul Berg, founder and director of the Schneider Male Chorus, passed away at age sixty-eight. Paul sang a number of solos at the memorial service held in the Humanities Theatre at the University of Waterloo. He praised his friend and mentor for his "kindly encouragement and guidance" in encouraging him to pursue a professional career.

22

A Turning Point

If Paul Frey was to name a turning point in his stalled career, his performance in Stuart Hamilton's Opera in Concert production of *Werther*, opposite Maureen Forrester, would surely be it.

He'd engaged Hamilton as a private vocal coach and the two got along well. The tenor was in good company, as Hamilton occasionally coached star contralto Maureen Forrester. Surely a Renaissance man, Hamilton also earned a living as a classically trained pianist. He had a reputation among the classical music set as an "ideas man," a "large thinker."

Hamilton had envisioned developing the "Opera in Concert" concept in Canada. Popular in Europe and the U.S., it offered to audiences less well-known and scarcely performed operas in a concert format. Musical accompaniment was limited to piano. Uncostumed performers would sing, with no acting involved. Usually each opera was performed only twice, with different casts each evening.

The first opera tagged for Hamilton's opening 1976 Opera in Concert was French composer Jules Massenet's *Werther*. And he had some star power in mind for the title roles.

Werther, written and composed in 1892, follows the journey of the poet hero of the same name. Set in the 1780's, the narrative follows Werther, who travels the countryside searching for true love. Meeting Charlotte, who is pledged in marriage to another, Werther despairs. Realizing only too late of her love for Werther, who by this time has sustained a mortal wound, Charlotte confesses her love.

Hamilton had piqued the interest of Forrester, then living and working in New York, for the role of Charlotte. Agreeable to the appearance, the contralto issued one advisement before she signed on: "Just get me a decent tenor to sing the *Werther* part." No problem for Hamilton! He had just the "decent tenor" for the job. Paul Frey, about to graduate from the University of Toronto Opera School—with no major performances to his credit—was his choice. Given Paul's continuing status as a lowly chorus member of both the Opera School and of the Canadian Opera Company, his selection to play the role opposite a star of Forrester's stature surely surprised many in the operatic world.

Forrester, on the other hand, had no doubts. She'd met Paul Frey twice, as a favor to Paul Berg during Paul's WLU Summer Music Workshop and had performed with him in the Kitchener-Waterloo Symphony production of *Carmen*. On both occasions, the forthright Forrester had praised and encouraged the young tenor. She did require him to audition for *Werther*, but was convinced of Paul Frey's capabilities.

Hamilton's concept for *Werther* saw two concerts with different casts. Forrester and Frey would sing the second of the two performances. This gave Paul an opportunity to critique the first from an audience seat at the St. Lawrence Centre for the Performing Arts. Frey's verdict was unequivocal. Although he could find no fault with the performers or the format—accompanied only by piano with no movement or costuming—he found it a dull medium. "I determined to do it in a more exciting way to make up for the lack of staging," he later acknowledged.

"In a more exciting way," Paul Frey's performance surely was. *Globe and Mail* music reviewer John Kraglund tells the tale: "Frey was a surprise to most of the audience. First noticed a few seasons ago in operatic concert performances with the Kitchener-Waterloo Symphony Orchestra, he has sung only minor roles with the COC . . . but the important thing is that he has a true ringing tenor voice and the stamina to last through a demanding role. It should not be long before he starts to attract a much wider attention."[36]

The surprises continued after the curtain came down. Stuart Hamilton himself recalls: ". . . and when they were to go on for their bows, Paul Frey, though his was the title role, refused to be the climactic last on the platform because, he said, 'I'm singing with Maureen Forrester, who, after all, is a star.'"[37]

The plot behind the scenes was rehearsed, Hamilton revealed. "Maureen quietly asked the stage manager, a very large, strong man, to wrap his arms around Frey and restrain him while Maureen skipped out for the second-last bow. As she came back offstage, passing a red-faced Frey, he was propelled by the stage manager for his proper final bow. Maureen muttered to him, 'The name of the opera is *Werther*, after all!'"³⁸

In his review, Blaik Kirby of the *Globe* went one step further than Kraglund and calls Paul Frey's performance ". . . of the most electrifying musical debuts that become the stuff of legend." "A month ago in Toronto," Kirby recounted, "there was one of those electrifying musical debuts that become the stuff of legend. An unknown tenor, fresh out of Opera School, appeared with the great Maureen Forrester and sang so well that he got a bigger ovation than she did."³⁹ Forrester herself, in the 1990 CBC series *Adrienne Clarkson Presents* on Paul Frey, praises the tenor: "He has a marvellous voice. It just pours out of him."⁴⁰

As graduation from the University of Toronto Opera School approached and with it Paul Frey's mounting collection of laudatory press clippings, he continued to feel wholly unfulfilled. "As I watched my classmates getting selected for solo roles in school productions and in the Canadian Opera Company performances, I continued where I'd been since first year—in the chorus."

A small solo part as Rinuccio in the Opera School's one-act spring 1976 production of the comic opera *Gianni Schicchi* was Paul's scant reward for his progress. W. J. Pitcher from the *Kitchener-Waterloo Record* had traveled to Toronto to review hometown boy Frey's performance and praised: "Mr. Frey's voice has gained a good deal of smoothness of delivery and uniformity of colouring throughout the range. The timbre has warmth and the top notes show more operatic-type punch and brilliance."⁴¹

From Paul's own point of view, comparing 1972, when he entered the school, to 1976, as he was about to graduate, he was a much-improved singer: "My abilities with language had greatly improved—especially Italian. French was still challenging. I count and read notes much better. My voice was stronger and richer and I'd gotten many positive comments about that. Still the Opera School and the Canadian Opera Company saw fit not to award me a solo role."

And so, in the spring of 1976, Paul Frey graduated from the University of Toronto Opera School. In three years, he'd never been tested as to whether he could carry a major role in a three-act opera. The "dumb tenor" and the "music illiterate" label that he'd been saddled with, at least in the eyes of

Part 5: Opera School: Odd Man Out

the opera establishment, had stuck. And it hurt. "I didn't leave a successful business behind to be a chorus singer," he had muttered to one journalist.

With restraint, (and surely still not wanting to burn bridges), to *Globe and Mail* reporter Kirby he praised the school for allowing him to remain for a year longer in the program. Controlling his disappointment, he only criticizes the school for "giving me few chances to shine."[42]

23

An American Road Trip

Paul Frey departed the University of Toronto Opera School without picking up his graduation diploma.[43] More than forty years later, he has no regrets. "I didn't think then, nor do I think now, that the school encouraged me, or did much for me. I fell by their wayside." Bass-baritone Dan Lichti, who attended the Opera School during Paul's last year, acknowledges the slight, and the effects it must have had at the time. "I feel badly that this happened to Paul and I admire how he responded."[44]

Not that Paul had had time to wool-gather about slights and disappointments. He'd engaged agent David Haber, former artistic director of the National Ballet of Canada, to represent him, and Haber did his job keeping Paul Frey employed. From Bach's *Passion* at the National Arts Centre in Ottawa, to *The Messiah* with the Kitchener-Waterloo Philharmonic Choir, to *L'Amore Dei Tre Re* with Opera in Concert, life was busy and the reviews were glowing. And then there was the upcoming Canadian Opera Company tour.

The winter of 1977 would see Paul and forty-five members of the COC, under the direction of conductor Timothy Vernon, on an ambitious 9,000-mile, fifty-six-performance road tour of the American Midwest and Western Canada. Traveling by coach, they'd be setting up at various high school auditoriums, community centers, and arenas across the two nations, staging performances of *La Traviata* and *La Bohème*. Paul had worked his way out of the chorus to take a lead role and would alternate with tenor Glyn Evans as Rodolpho in *La Bohème* and as Alfred in *La Traviata*.

Booking agents Columbia Artist Management of New York were guaranteeing the Company $45,000 per production. The Canadian Department of External Affairs had also contributed to the costs.

Across Middle America, reviews for the Canadians were uniformly glowing. One reviewer called the COC "the best touring company in America." (Did Canada have opera singers too!) Another fan called the company "uniformly excellent." Tenor Paul Frey in the role of Alfred in *La Traviata* was described by reviewer Terence O'Grady as "a dashing figure with a natural and flexible tenor voice."[45] Writer Jack Rudolph's review in the Green Bay, Wisconsin *News Chronicle* calls *La Traviata* "the best in twenty years" and compliments Paul Frey's voice as "big and resonant with a fine tenoric ping."[46]

Paul carries warm memories of the gruelling odyssey. He recalls pulling into Madison, Wisconsin during a bitter cold snap where temperatures dipped to negative forty degrees Fahrenheit. "People would comment about the weather they were having and more than one would say: 'if it's forty degrees below here in Wisconsin I can't imagine how much colder it is way up in Canada.' Of course they had no idea that Toronto was much further south than Wisconsin! If it was Canada, it was the land of snow and ice!"

One memory only broke the spell of success. And that didn't come until the group's return to Toronto. "When I got off the tour bus, Linda was there to meet me and she was holding Ben, who was about three. I went right over to give them a hug and Ben turned away from me. He was young enough that he didn't recognize me. Oh that really hurt!"

24

Back to the Status Quo

It was a weary Canadian Opera Company that had returned to Toronto in late February 1977. But after a day or so of family time, Paul picked up where he had left off before the American tour. *Globe and Mail* reviewer Kraglund, commenting on the company's, and in particular Paul Frey's, Toronto Opera in Concert performance of *Il Corsano* noted that his voice was "less splendid elsewhere . . . not due to loss of style or effort but just back from COC touring and his voice sometimes lost its ringing quality."[47]

The New Year also brought the end of a drought. Five years after he'd enrolled in Opera School, Paul Frey finally had his first starring full-length role for a performance in Ontario. Mounted by the Toronto Opera Repertoire and staged at Toronto's Central Technical School, he starred as the Duke of Mantua in Verdi's *Rigoletto*. Unfortunately, no press releases or reviews mark the long-awaited occasion.

Oratorio performances, including those with the London, Ontario and Kingston Symphony Orchestras filled up Paul's booking calendar over the winter. An April invitation to sing Handel's *Messiah* with the Memorial University Festival Choir and Orchestra gave him his first trip to Newfoundland.

And Paul Frey wasn't so much the 'big-city" performer to turn down a spring invitation from the Brantford Music Club's Young Artist's Recital. June saw him also as a special guest at his home church, St. Jacobs Mennonite's Service of Praise and Dedication.

Being busy had financial benefits. "I was earning around $25,000 a year from my singing engagements," he recalls. "And that was a very good salary back then." Then there was the delight of being a father to Ben, now a toddler.

Part 5: Opera School: Odd Man Out

Still, Paul didn't feel completely fulfilled. "I felt I had more to give, more to achieve than singing in one-act operas and in oratorio. I still hadn't had a role offered to me by a major opera company. And that frustrated me." His frustration was shared by others in his situation—talented Canadian artists, with big dreams, living in a country with a painfully brief and underdeveloped opera season. And when that season was limited to only three to four major Canadian cities—Toronto, Ottawa, Montreal, and Vancouver—the opportunities and roles were few. Major stars like Maureen Forrester, John Vickers, and Louis Quilico went out of the country to build their careers. Paul began to wonder if that would need to be his route. With a young family, it would be tough, but . . .

In Ottawa, performing in a minor role at the National Arts Centre, Paul vented his frustration to Mario Bernardi, artistic director of the NAC's summer opera festival. Their conversation of more than forty years past bears eavesdropping:

Paul Frey: "Why won't you give me a major role in a production? I've proven myself over and over again."

Mario Bernardi: "I can't give you a major role because you don't have experience in a starring role. You don't have a track record in a starring role. When the season is as short as is it in Canada, then you can't go with unknown and untested singers."

Paul Frey: "You say I need experience. I agree. Then how do I get experience if you or other artistic directors won't hire me in a role? I need someone to give me a chance."

Mario Bernardi: "You'll probably have to go to Europe to get the experience you need."

Paul Frey: "And how do I get that experience in Europe?"

It was at this point that the penny dropped.

Part 6

European Adventure: Steeling Himself to Fail

(1977–1978)

25

The Canada Council Offers a Chance

The Massey Commission, undertaken by the Canadian federal government in 1951, had painted a bleak picture of the arts in this country. Among its other findings, the commission (named for its chair, and future Canadian governor-general, Vincent Massey) found that:

Professional theater was "moribund"; musical life was largely confined to church basements and school gymnasia; professional artistic ventures were few in number and almost non-existent outside the largest cities. In an entire year, English Canada produced only fourteen works of fiction.

Six years after the commission's findings, in 1956, the Canada Council for the Arts was created and was funded from the estates of two wealthy industrialists, Sir James Dunn and Izaak Walton Killam.

The Council, which was overseen by the Canadian Parliament, aimed "to foster and promote the study and enjoyment of, and the production of works in, the arts." The Canada Council's first senior arts officer was David P. Silcox of Toronto.

As it has for over sixty years, the Canada Council for the Arts continues to provide grants and services to professional Canadian artists and arts organizations in dance, interdisciplinary arts, media arts, music, opera, theater, writing, publishing and the visual arts.[48]

IN 1977, AMONG THE Canada Council grants available for Canadian artists was one directed at those heading towards a professional operatic career. Advertised widely on bulletin boards at the University of Toronto Opera School, and at other similar institutions across Canada, the program offered

Part 6: European Adventure: Steeling Himself to Fail

classically trained singers an opportunity to further their career in Europe through an audition tour.

Candidates for the program were invited to send in applications to be considered. And while paper credentials would allow applicants to move on to the next stage, they would need to audition before a jury of professionals in both academic and performance fields. This would determine who would be chosen for the all-expenses-paid audition tour of several European opera houses, each looking to hire talent.

With Mario Bernardi's advice, "you'll need to go to Europe to move up," ringing in his ears, Paul applied for Canada Council program. After due consideration, his application was approved. He now prepared for the audition of a lifetime. He wanted to get it right: selection, presentation and, of course, voice.

Paul recalls his state of mind in the days leading up to his Canada Council audition. "I was earning about $25,000 a year from my performances in Canada and my Timothy Eaton Church contract. That was very good money then for a freelance opera singer. I was busy and I never had problems getting jobs. Plus I was settled in Toronto with a wife and son. So, why was I not satisfied with that? Why was I looking to Europe?"

He looks to his family background to explain what drove him. "My father had wanted to be the best he could be in his field—that was in farming and agricultural trucking. He started with one truck and had built it up to the place where, when I took over a successful business, he had three vehicles. I guess I learned from him to push myself—to climb up the ladder as far as I could."

And in 1977, for Paul Frey, that ladder led to Europe. Had he been singing major parts in full-length operas staged in Canada, Paul may not have looked to faraway Europe. "But I wasn't; I was getting lots of jobs singing oratorio and minor parts in opera, but not lead roles at home. And that made all the difference."

Fifteen applicants, including Paul Frey, from across Canada had been selected to sing for the Canada Council jury. Each was prepared to present two selections. Paul had conferred with his friend and Opera in Concert director Stuart Hamilton for advice, and would be singing an aria from the German opera *Der Freischütz* by German composer Carl Maria von Weber. His second selection, from Mozart's *Don Giovanni*, would be sung

The Canada Council Offers a Chance

in Italian. "I felt that both these selections showed my voice off to its best quality," Paul explains.

The day of the Canada Council audition found Paul playing host to a number of stomach butterflies. "But then I never felt I did well during auditions," he states. "I was always better and stronger during the performance." Still, he had confidence that he stood a strong chance of being selected. Heaven's knows he'd had enough practice auditioning for jobs.

26

One of Five

PAUL FREY'S HOMETOWN FANS found out the results of the Canada Council audition thanks to music columnist W. J. Pitcher in the *Kitchener-Waterloo Record*. The article titled "Tenor Paul Frey Chosen: 5 Canadians win auditions in Europe" announced the results of the Canada Council competition. Along with Frey, soprano Anna Chornodolska of Montreal, tenor David Smith of Vancouver, soprano Lynn Channing of Newfoundland, and soprano Lois Marsh of Montreal were given the nod. No basses, baritones, or mezzo-sopranos were among the number.[49]

Plans called for the group to leave Toronto for Vienna, Austria on October 20, 1977. Edith Binnie, publicity officer with the Faculty of Music at the University of Toronto, would travel with the five hopefuls. She would make the first connection with opera agent Ioan Holender in Vienna. All five would perform their repertoire for Holender. Then they would carry on to sing again for another agent in Munich, Germany. After conferring, the agents would direct the Canadians on to one or more opera houses to audition for a position.

It was a well-coordinated exercise, designed to give Canadian opera hopefuls an opportunity for regular employment in the field they had chosen to make their living. With the dearth of opportunities in Canada, this was chance of a lifetime.

Selection of their operatic selection for the European agents would be key. For the same reasons as for his Canada Council audition, Paul would sing von Weber's *Der Freischütz* in German and Mozart's *Don Giovanni* in Italian. Both pieces, he felt, would showcase his strong tenor voice. The choice of two languages would demonstrate his versatility and adaptability. (Paul chose not to sing in French for the agents!)

It was an upbeat group of Canadian opera hopefuls who arrived in Vienna for what, if successful, could be their big break. One, at least, by far the oldest in the group, felt supremely confident now that the first hurdle was over. "I was fairly positive that I'd be offered a contract from somebody," states Paul. He'd prepared well for his big break and his selections impressed agent Holender. But he recalls his surprise in hearing Holender's comment: "I see that you are a Mozart tenor." "I never really thought of myself that way, but if that was the agent saw me then I wasn't going to argue."

Having performed—and well, he thought—Paul awaited his instructions. For the most part, he (and the four other Canadians) would now be on their own. Each would follow their own route to the auditions (per agents' instructions), although in some cases their journeys would overlap. Both being tenors, David Smith and Paul Frey might sing at the same audition call.

Travel from city to city would be by train. It was a new experience for country boy Frey. "I hadn't traveled all that much, especially in Europe, so I was nervous until I got the hang of train travel, which is very convenient in Europe."

Paul's schedule over the coming two to three weeks would see him auditioning at six different opera houses in three countries: Salzburg, Austria; Braunschweig, Wuppertal, and Auchen in Germany; and on to St. Galen and Basel in Switzerland. His itinerary was coordinated to meet opera houses' audition calls, not geographical proximity to one another. Paul's route would see him zigzagging from Braunschweig, Germany to Salzburg, Austria, up to Wuppertal, Germany, south to St. Galen, Switzerland, northwest to Auchen, Germany, and finally to Basel, Switzerland. "So I spent a lot of time on the train seeing the countryside."

He was glad when he and Vancouverite David Smith could share a train seat. Traveling time allowed them to compare notes. "David's selections were both fairly short, so in most cases after he finished the first, he'd be asked to sing the second. The result was that the jury had two opportunities to see what he could do. My first selection, *Der Freischütz*, was quite long so usually I only got to sing one." Paul hoped he'd made the right choice. Oh well, far too late for making adjustments.

As audition number one segued into audition two and three, the sense of adventure that Paul had felt in anticipating the tour was gradually being replaced by exhaustion and stress. "You'd get to the audition and there

Part 6: European Adventure: Steeling Himself to Fail

might be up to thirty other singers there. All for the same reason. You'd sing, on a lighted stage, in a darkened hall with the jury seated somewhere in the audience—you never got to see their faces. Somebody would say: 'Thanks, we'll be in touch if we want you.' And the next singer was up to bat. It didn't take me long to become very disillusioned by it. By the fifth audition I was ready to pack my bags and go home."

It was during these gray days that Paul began to doubt the course on which he had set out. "I'd say to myself: 'Why am I doing this? I have a satisfying career in Canada; I'm busy and making money. So why am I putting myself through this stress?'" He'd understate his feelings during phone conversations with Linda at home. "I wasn't anxious to share failure."

Close to cutting the European experience short, and being a "no-show" for the *Stadttheatre Basel* audition, the last stop on his operatic magical mystery tour, Paul realized that his plane ticket home couldn't be exchanged for an earlier one. And so Paul Frey, tenor, age thirty-six, former agricultural truck driver from St. Clements, Ontario, decided to finish what he had started.

He had no doubt that at this last stop, as had been the case with the previous five, he'd sing, be thanked for his efforts, and hear: "We'll be in touch." After that inevitable message, he'd pack his bags and head for the airport. That was OK. He had a full schedule of performances ahead of him at home.

"So I set out for the Basel audition feeling very relaxed and mellow," recalls Paul. "I had no pressure on me and was just finishing my obligations as a courtesy to Edith Binney and the Canada Council people."

It seems that fate had different plans in store.

27

Finishing What He Had Started

WHAT PAUL COULD NOT have known when he arrived to audition at the *Stadttheatre Basel* was that there had been some internal changes taking place in theater management. There was a new theater manager, (intendant) Horst Statkus, and under him some long-time artists' contracts had been terminated. This man at the top was looking for fresh new faces and voices.

As such, the top tenor, an Eastern European performer, found himself looking for new employment in early November 1977. An audition was scheduled to find his replacement. Among the thirty-odd aspirants was a "relaxed and mellow" Canadian, Paul Frey. Little could he have been aware of the effects of his state of mind on his performance.

"Mr. Paul Frey." The door to the theater had opened. As with the other auditions, the *Stadttheatre* jury was seated throughout the darkened concert hall and Paul took his place on the stage. Delivering *Der Freischütz* with confidence, he was pleased to be asked to carry on to his second selection, *Don Giovanni*. That hadn't happened at every audition.

Halfway through, he was told to stop. "Here it goes again—I'm done," he muttered to himself. Relieved that the interminable audition tour was finally at an end, he turned to leave and was stopped in his tracks: "Please wait in the canteen; we'd like to have a few words with you . . ." The voice came from somewhere in the darkened concert hall.

Paul joined five other hopefuls (of approximately thirty tenors auditioning) in the theater cafeteria. He recalls his thoughts during his reprieve: "It wasn't what I had expected. And it did throw me a bit. I had been directing my thoughts to home and my future there." One by one, the other candidates were called into an adjoining conference room. One by one they

Part 6: European Adventure: Steeling Himself to Fail

emerged, clearly disappointed. "A couple of them were in tears," Paul recalls of that day.

Then, finally: "Paul Frey."

"I remember the scene as if it was yesterday," Paul offers, with a smile. Seated behind a table were the *Stadttheatre* "bigwigs," including the new intendant, Statkus; his next-in-command, orchestra conductor Armin Jordan; the theater's head vocal coach, Rainer Altorfer; and the theater stage director, Martin Markun.

There were no introductory pleasantries in this meeting. Out of the mouth of Statkus came the startling invitation: "We'd like to offer you a two-year contract to begin in the fall of 1978." Paul was thunderstruck. On the verge of returning home empty-handed twenty-four hours previously, he'd been offered the silver cup. "They asked if I could return the next day—all hotel and meal expenses covered—to discuss the details. I agreed."

But before he left, management had one question they'd like answered. "There will be three new operas staged over the 1978–1979 season: *Fidelio*, *Werther*, and *The Bartered Bride*. We'd expect that you would do two: *The Bartered Bride* and either *Fidelio* or *Werther*. If you accept our offer, which one would you like to do?"

Paul laughs at the memory: "With my energetic farm boy background I said: 'Well that's a difficult decision; I like both very much so I'd like to do both *Werther* and *Fidelio*!" Paul's response was unexpected, but seemed to please the Basel jury. "Could you sing them for us when you return tomorrow?" He could and he would.

Returning to his hotel, enveloped in the sweet smell of success, Paul thought back to hearing Beethoven's *Fidelio* for the first time. He had been laid up with a hockey injury—chastising himself for giving his time to the beloved game, and soothing his angsts by listening to opera.

"I'd come across some recordings, including one by Canadian tenor Jon Vickers singing the role of Florestan in *Fidelio*. From that moment on, I was hooked, entranced, and I tried to fashion my voice singing the role after his."

In the chorus of the Canadian Opera Company he'd sung in *Fidelio* too. But what now was placed before him was the lead. "This was Florestan! Being able to sing it was a dream come true."

Finishing What He Had Started

Paul's first call on leaving the theater was to his wife, Linda, at home in Toronto. Then, over the coming hours, contemplating the gargantuan step that his career had taken, Paul mulled over a myriad of thoughts. "It was exciting, for sure. If I took the offer, we'd be going from a comfortable life in Canada, close to family and friends, to something completely different. Our son was happy and looking forward to starting kindergarten in Toronto. And my career was doing well there—financially and otherwise. To give up all that to move to Europe was a huge step in our lives. And what if it didn't work out? What if we weren't happy?"

On the other hand, there were a million reasons why he *should* accept the offer—the least of which was the opportunity to sing at the *Stadttheatre Basel*. It was a well-respected, second-tier European opera house in a cosmopolitan European city. "I might have been more uncertain if I'd been offered a contract from a city like Wuppertal," states Paul. "It was quite provincial, with primarily German the language spoken." Basel, due to it being a center for the pharmaceutical industry, was a diverse European city with German, English, and French heard—on the street and in the opera.

Over the next hours, he mulled over the gift that had been handed to him. "It was such a huge step—and a bit frightening too. But why would I turn it down? Unless what I heard tomorrow didn't sit well, I'd accept the contract, with gladness."

28

Sorting It Out

PAUL SET OUT FOR the *Stadttheatre* the next day walking on air, confident in the decision that he had made. He would accept the offer. The financial details would be handled by his new agent, Ioan Holender in Vienna. He'd negotiate the performance end with the theater management.

His interest in singing lead tenor in both *Fidelio* and *Werther* remained, but he'd comply with their decision. They'd take close note of his voice capabilities as he sang excerpts from both operas. *Fidelio* was usually handled by a tenor in the dramatic tenor *Fach*, Werther primarily by tenors who specialize in the lyric *Fach*.

A brief lesson in "*Fachs* 101" is helpful in understanding operatic voice requirements (particularly for the tenor voice).[50]

The Fach system of operatic voice classification was developed by German opera houses in the late 1800's. The system assisted companies in casting for roles within the opera.[51] *A nation that loved order, even when it came to operatic voice, Germany placed various registers in six broad categories. Further differentiation was made within each of these categories.*

Voice characteristics were studied with reference to: range, weight, timbre, vocal register, and other subtleties. Age, physical build, and experience also figured into the Fach categorization. On the basis of this, operatic singers were placed in a particular Fach and would audition for parts that suited their voice characteristic. Auditions would be limited to those whose voices were appropriate.

Sorting It Out

For the tenor range there are three primary Fach classifications: lyric tenor, dramatic tenor, and heroic or heldentenor. The voice of the lyric tenor is of a higher range and lighter tone, described by some as warm and flexible. Roles for the lyric tenor include Don Octavio in Don Giovanni, *Werther in* Werther, *and Alfredo in* La Traviata. *Range is from low C to high C.*

The dramatic tenor's tone is larger and more powerful than the lyric, with extended range. Roles for dramatic tenors include Don Jose in Bizet's Carmen, *Lohengrin in Wagner's* Lohengrin, *and Florestan in* Fidelio. *Range is from low C to high C.*

The heldentenor (or heroic tenor) deserves special consideration. Some opera scholars differentiate the dramatic tenor and the heldentenor not by voice but by genre. That being, the dramatic tenor is a product of Italian opera; the heldentenor of German opera. With baritone facility in the middle range of voice, the heldentenor can "pierce" through the orchestra sound. Examples are Tristan in Tristan und Isolde *and Othello in* Othello. *Heldentenor range is from B below low C to high C.*

At age thirty-six, with only six years of opera training behind him, Paul describes his own voice: "At that point, I was more comfortable with the lyric range. And my voice hadn't yet developed that 'ping' of the dramatic or lyric tenor." (The characteristic ping allowed tenors to shoot their voice past the large orchestras which were a characteristic of German opera, especially Wagnerian.)

Paul was satisfied with his performance before theater management, and awaited their reaction. "I would have been disappointed if they had picked one or the other. I was eager to sing both." He need not to have worried. "You're right," offered intendant Statkus. "You *can* sing both. And so you will." *The Bartered Bride* by Smetana would make up the third opera for the 1978–1979 season.

Basel management was surely also rubbing their hands in glee, contracting such a versatile performer. If the voice of their new Canadian star had not been adaptable enough to sing both operas, the theater would have had to hire an outside tenor. "They were delighted to have someone like me," says Paul. "I was saving them money!"

An operetta or two was also on the theater's playbill for the 1978–1979 season. "Operettas are not as prestigious as the full opera," states Paul, "and most opera singers won't sing them. But me? I was happy to do this too.

Part 6: European Adventure: Steeling Himself to Fail

The more I could sing, the happier I was!" And so, Johann Strauss's *A Night in Venice* was added to Paul Frey's repertoire for the 1977–1978 season. There'd be no extra pay for this addition. "I was paid a set salary whether I did one opera or two or three a year, or added an operetta."

He'd bask in the warmth of having a regular home life too. Freelance life in Canada had been unpredictable. One weekend in Thunder Bay, then back to Brantford for a midweek gig, then east to Montreal the coming Saturday. As a salaried employee of the *Stadttheatre Basel*, he'd have a regular schedule—so regular it would be posted on a performance bulletin board.

It would be jam-packed too. Over the 1978–1979 season, the three operas: *Fidelio*, *Werther*, and *The Bartered Bride* would be performed. Six weeks of rehearsal for *Fidelio* would be followed by opening night. By this time, rehearsals for *Werther* would begin. Once opening night for *Werther* was under their belt, performers and musicians would begin rehearsals for *The Bartered Bride*. All fitting nicely into a ten-month opera season.

Paul left his meeting fairly floating on air. He'd gained insight into the form that his life would take when he returned to take up his contract a year from now. "And I liked what I heard." He'd be expected back in Basel by late summer of 1978 when rehearsals would begin. Arrangements for accommodation and other fine details would come directly and through agent Holender.

Returning to Vienna, where he would catch a flight home to Toronto, Paul Frey could feel only relief and unbridled anticipation. "If I hadn't gotten a contract in Europe, I would have resumed my life as it had been. But this was so much more exciting."

What began as an adventure in late summer had afforded a prize. "I'd worked long and hard for this and it hadn't been easy—especially during Opera School and the COC, where I'd not been given the opportunities others had been given."

On the flight home, he chuckled to himself how close he had come to not attending the Basel auditions. And that would have been a cruel irony. "At the beginning of the tour when I'd been given the list of the six audition cities, I'd picked Basel as the one I'd choose if I had the chance. It was a world-class city with world-class opportunities to sing opera—in Italian, French, and German. It would have been much harder to develop a

Sorting It Out

reputation in cities like Wuppertal and Braunschweig, where only German was spoken and was the main language of the opera."

Some dreams do come true. Paul Frey's was surely one.

29

Ten-Month Home Interlude

THERE WAS LITTLE DOWN time to reflect on his European coup once Paul returned to Toronto in November. He had a full slate of bookings to keep him in fine voice before he returned to Basel in late July 1978.

Paul launched into them with the same work ethic and enthusiasm as he'd carried throughout his earlier Canadian career. "I had a job to do, and would do it to the very best of my ability." No let-up on travel either. He could handle that. "I'd always enjoyed traveling across Canada, singing in a variety of theaters, in different cities, as I got to discover areas of Canada I'd never seen before."

If there was any change in him, it referenced only his newfound confidence. "After I got the Basel contract and came home, now when I walked into a Canadian concert hall I had more confidence than I'd shown before." He'd surely caused more than a few of his colleagues who'd toiled with him in the COC chorus to take notice too. "Many congratulated me; some were jealous."

And what was he looking forward to once his new life in Basel, Switzerland kicked into gear? "It was getting the chance to sing one role over and over again—twenty times or more—growing into it and perfecting it. That was something I'd not had in my Canadian career." A long run in Canada was maybe three performances. "The most I'd ever repeated a role was when I was on the COC tour through the U.S."

The Basel contract had also given him a growing sense of security in the uncertain entertainment world. "It was so hard to make a living as a Canadian opera singer; few made it—Jon Vickers and later Ben Heppner are exceptions. Many who stayed in Canada eventually moved into teaching."

Ten-Month Home Interlude

Such was the direction of another Waterloo County opera and oratorio singer, Dan Lichti. After his brief year at Opera School in Toronto, Lichti had studied with Theo Lindenbaum in Detmold, Germany. Beginning his professional career in 1974 at the Stratford Festival, he went on to build a stellar concert and oratorio career across Canada, the U.S., and Europe. In 1998 he accepted a position as Associate Professor and Coordinator of Voice for the Faculty of Music at Wilfrid Laurier University in Waterloo, Ontario. He remained there while taking opera engagements until his retirement from WLU in 2017. But that kind of a future wasn't in Paul Frey's crystal ball.

The final weeks of what had turned out to be a banner year, 1977, were packed. Engagements with the K-W Symphony's *Requiem* by Verdi and Handel's *Messiah* with the Toronto Symphony closed out the year.

The New Year of 1978 opened with a performance with the Mississauga Symphony. That was followed by Opera in Concert's *Romeo and Juliet* by Gounod and Verdi's *Stiffelio*. A long-overdue invitation came from the Canadian Opera Company with his first starring role. He took the role of Alfredo in the eleven-performance run of Verdi's *La Traviata* at the Royal Alexandra Theatre. Former conductor of the Kitchener-Waterloo Symphony, Raffi Armenian led the Toronto Symphony.

The *Globe and Mail*'s music critic John Kraglund, who'd followed Paul Frey's career since University of Toronto Opera School days (a critic given to reserve over the gushing *Kitchener-Waterloo Record*'s W. J. Pitcher), was congratulatory in his review of Paul's performance. "If his [Frey's] dramatic ability still leaves room for polishing he was rarely guilty of overplaying his role. Vocally he had some splendid moments . . . As the opera progressed there were occasions when phrases would slip out of context with a sound that was closer to crooning than Verdi style. It was nevertheless an impressive major debut."[52]

Spring brought a concert with the hometown Menno Singers and the K-W Symphony Orchestra. Also he journeyed to Thunder Bay, taking the lead role of P. F. Pinkerton in Puccini's *Madama Butterfly*.

Meanwhile on the home front, the Freys had put their Toronto home up for sale and stored their furniture. A fan of upscale automobiles since his teenage years, Paul had purchased a Mercedes-Benz. With all the details—color, model, bells and whistles, and price—dealt with in Toronto,

Part 6: European Adventure: Steeling Himself to Fail

the Freys could pick up their new vehicle right from the factory in Stuttgart, Germany when they returned in late July 1978. They'd make the final 170-kilometer journey to Basel by luxury car.

Over the passing months, Paul had reflected on the "what comes next" after his two-year Basel contract was fulfilled. "I always saw myself returning to Canada and to opera here—eventually. But I'd expect to be singing bigger, lead roles, and earning a larger salary. I also saw myself singing in the U.S."

That had been given promise earlier that year after a successful audition in New York. He'd been offered a role in the Strauss opera *Ariadne auf Naxos*, which would open in Kansas City. "I was flattered but really didn't give it that much consideration. My immediate future was in Basel, so I turned the U.S. down." Paul was sure there'd be more where that came from after Europe—however long that would be.

"I usually went on five-year plans in my life," he reveals. "Five years from the time I entered Opera School to leaving for Basel. I'd hopefully try Europe for five years, then evaluate at the end of that." Whatever materialized, Paul had an abiding faith that it would work out. It just would!

Part 7

A New Life in Basel

(1978–1979)

30

On Their Way

THE FREY FAMILY—PAUL, LINDA, and little Ben, age four—boarded a plane for Stuttgart, Germany in August 1978. Ahead was Paul's future, and surely a mountain of adventure.

Waiting at the Mercedes-Benz factory in Stuttgart was the family's new vehicle. Paul was elated. Like his father, he'd been luxury car fan since his early driving days. Then it was traveling southwest the 170-odd kilometers toward their new home in Basel, Switzerland. Excitement was mixed with elation and a skiff of anxiety for the road ahead. A "run-in" with Swiss authorities at the German-Swiss border soon brought the carefree mood to earth. Paul explains:

"Car seats for children weren't compulsory in Canada in 1978 and so Ben was sitting on Linda's knee in the front seat. But Switzerland is a very strict and careful nation. So children needed to be buckled in." The Freys were told, in no uncertain terms, that they *could not* proceed without a car seat for the little guy. Negotiations between the authorities and the Canadians continued for several moments. They were only allowed to proceed with a promise to acquire the proper child safety equipment immediately on arrival in Basel.

It was a telling introduction to the Swiss natural character—precise, efficient, and by the rules.

It wouldn't be a hardship for the Frey family acclimatizing to the beautiful and cosmopolitan city of Basel. Switzerland's third largest city, after Zurich and Geneva, Basel's population in the late 1970's hovered around

Part 7: A New Life in Basel

180,000 people. With 40 percent of its inhabitants foreigners, the city's cosmopolitan reputation was well-deserved. Swiss-German (High German) was the official language spoken, with Basel-German the main language on the street. French, Italian, and English could be heard throughout the city too.

By the mid to late twentieth century, Basel had emerged as an important commercial center for the chemical and pharmaceutical industries. The city also ranked as having one of the highest standards of living in the world. Politically, the country was stable and advanced. Home to the University of Basel, founded in 1460, for centuries, Basel has served as a safe haven from political unrest outside Switzerland. And culturally, Basel boasted a number of world-class museums, including the *Kunstmuseum*. In 1660, it was the first museum in the world to open its collection to the public.

The *Stadttheatre Basel* reflected all that was modern and well planned in the city. It too had a distinguished history. Designed by Swiss architect Melchior Berri, this municipal or city theater was founded in 1834. Work on a new theater began in 1873, with it opening in 1875. Fire destroyed the building in 1904, and it would be five years before its replacement was opened. In 1975, just three years before Paul Frey's arrival, a modern new theater was built.

An intendant or general manager headed the theater. Horst Statkus, who had claimed the role just before Paul's arrival in 1978, was the *Stadttheatre Basel*'s twelfth intendant. Armin Jordan was the head conductor of Basel's two orchestras. Paul Frey would quickly become Jordan's most favored singer.

Opera was only one of the performing arts presented at the *Stadttheatre*. Ballet, dramatic, and musical theater productions were also produced year-round. The theater boasted not one, but two symphony orchestras.

The theater employed 400 people, including both performers and staff. With the majority of them European, British and Americans were part of the complement too. Canadians? They were a rare breed. Paul Frey would join a complement of professional opera singers: baritones and basses, tenors, sopranos, mezzo-sopranos, and contraltos. Each range would have its own principal singer, with others taking minor or character roles, as well as singing in the chorus. As principal "house" tenor, Paul would sing frequently with Romanian soprano Maria Slatinaru.

31

Getting Settled and Learning the Ropes

THE THEATER HAD ARRANGED for the Frey family to stay temporarily in one of the three furnished apartments that were part of the complex. Out-of-town guests and employees who were in transition were accommodated there until they were able to make arrangements for more permanent lodgings. Within six weeks, the Freys had found a suitable apartment complex. A number of Americans also lived on the site, including one family with two young boys. This contact helped Linda and young Ben find their way around Basel.

With Paul's contract being of a two-year duration, they'd be keeping their eyes and ears open for a house to rent—preferably outside Basel. Living in bustling Toronto first, and smaller Basel presently, had done nothing to convince either Paul or Linda Frey that rural life was not preferable when raising a child.

As he was about to begin his European career, at age thirty-seven, Paul Frey describes his trained voice. "I'd say I was comfortable with the higher tenor range. Where some tenors like Jon Vickers avoided the high C, I didn't have to. I could make it fairly easily. But would I call myself a pure lyric tenor? No, I think my voice was in the middle range between a lighter, airier lyric tenor and a deeper, darker heroic tenor or heldentenor."

Paul goes on to explain that the voice of the dramatic tenor *grabs* the vocal chords. He credits Louis Quilico, his coach at the University of Toronto Opera School, for developing that treasure—one he says was still developing at this point in his career.

Part 7: A New Life in Basel

His first performance in Basel would be Beethoven's *Fidelio*, a romantic drama and the composer's only opera. He had sung *Fidelio* in the chorus of a COC production, but now the spotlight was on him in the title role of Florestan. Considered a timeless role for a dramatic tenor, the libretto is sung in German.

Beethoven worked on Fidelio between 1805 and 1814. Inspired by a true-to-life story from the French Revolution, the libretto (text or story line) revolves around a woman, Leonore, and her efforts to free her husband, Florestan, who is incarcerated unjustly in a deep and dark dungeon at the bottom of a prison. Dressed as a man and assuming the identity of Fidelio, a gaoler, Leonore sets out to free her beloved Florestan.

Dramatic tension rises as Marzelline, the daughter of the corrupt gaoler Don Pizzaro, falls in love with the imposter Fidelio and rejects her fiancé. Fidelio (Leonore's) efforts to free Florestan are ultimately rewarded and the evil Don Pizzaro is exposed as a villain.

Beethoven's opera remains an enduring love story, a favorite with both singers and audiences around the world. Written over two centuries ago, Fidelio's themes of the preciousness of liberty and of justice prevailing remain timeless.

In retrospect, having assumed the roles of hundreds of operatic characters over decades of performing, Paul places *Fidelio* near the top of his most favored. "The story is such a meaningful one, of love and endurance and hope. So many of the opera story lines are silly; *Fidelio* is not."

Six weeks of morning and early evening rehearsals began shortly after Paul arrived in Basel. He remembers his welcome from the cast and crew as a warm one, with the occasional touch of resentment. "I was aware that some members of the company, especially a few in the chorus—singers who had stayed in that role for some years—were unhappy that a Canadian had been hired over one of them." Any feelings of resentment were soon quashed once the Canadian opened his mouth on stage!

The cast of *Fidelio* was a multinational one. Florestan, the lead tenor, was sung by Canadian Paul Frey; Leonore, the lead female, was played by Romanian soprano Maria Slatinaru. African-American baritone Alan Evans sang villain Don Pizzaro. A multitude of other Europeans, mostly German-speaking, filled the rest.

Getting Settled and Learning the Ropes

Before the cast worked together in rehearsal, individual practice, at least for the lead parts, took the form of private sessions with a *Studienleiter* or a role coach. Paul differentiates these talented professionals from voice coaches such as Douglas Campbell and Victor Martens. "Once you got to this level, you were expected to have the voice necessary to perform your role. But studio coaches looked after the diction and expression among other things. If you pronounced a word incorrectly, they corrected you; if you sang a wrong note—you were tutored for this too."

In preparation for his role of Florestan, Paul worked with Basel *Studienleiter* Paul Zeltner. Sessions together would perfect the Canadian's pronunciation as well as his intonation and dramatic expression.[53] Paul felt himself at an advantage beginning his professional career with a German-language opera over an Italian or French one. Growing up speaking Pennsylvania Dutch (similar to High German, at least in its "harsh" consonant sound), he'd also taken conversational German during his aborted plans to study with Professor Lindenbaum.

Still, work—hard and long—was Paul Frey's recipe for achievement. The cast also jelled well in group rehearsal and the results were positive. Reviews for Paul Frey in the role of Florestan were glowing. He would count *Fidelio* as one of his most meaningful roles in his large operatic repertoire.

32

Bargaining with the Boss

WITHIN THREE PERFORMANCES OF *Fidelio*, a success by all accounts, Paul was called into intendant Statkus's office. The boss had something he'd like to propose to his star tenor. "We'd like to extend your two-year contract to a three-year one," he offered. "Everyone is delighted with the job you are doing and we'd like to keep you for an extra year, at least."

A quick study, Paul had only a few seconds to take in this invitation. "Of course they wanted me to stay an extra year," says Paul, "given my versatility. I was saving them the expense of hiring another tenor. And I was willing to sing operettas too." He asked for a day to think the offer over. Once at home, Paul and Linda took stock of their situation, financially.

"We'd left Canada with little luggage—pretty well one suitcase each," recalls Paul. "So we had to buy everything—furniture, dishes, bedding, even food staples. We bought a lot of it secondhand, as the thought was that we'd be only here for two years." But it hadn't taken the Freys long to observe that it was considerably more expensive to live in Switzerland than in Canada.

Paul's salary was higher than he'd earned in Canada, and he was aware that he was earning more than singers in comparable second or third-tier opera houses in Germany. The difference was that Basel had a higher cost of living index than either Canada or Germany. "So my dollars didn't go as far."

He'd contacted the Basel bank where he'd opened an account to ask for a loan. "They turned me down!" Paul chuckles at yet one more example of Swiss caution and reserve. "The worry was that as I was a foreigner I might skip the country without paying the loan back!" So the opportunity to talk to his boss about his contract couldn't have come at a better time. We'll

Bargaining with the Boss

listen in on the conversation as Paul enters intendant Horst Statkus's office to talk "contract":

Paul: "Leider kann ich einer Verlängerung meines Zweijahresvertrages nicht zustimmen. Ich hätte gerne einen neuen Dreijahresvertrag mit einer Gehaltserhöhung, da die Lebenshaltungskosten in Basel höher sind. Meine Familie hat Scwierigkeiten über die Runde zu kommen."

"No, I can't agree to an extension of my two-year contract. I would like you to tear up the old contract and draw up a three-year one, with a raise in pay. I'm finding that with the high cost of living here in Basel, my family is having trouble making ends meet."

Intendant: "Das können wir leider nicht Machen!"

"We can't do that!"

Paul: "Dann kann ich leider nicht zustimmen."

"Then I can't agree to your request."

At this point the conversation segues to Paul's luxury Mercedes-Benz, resplendent in the parking lot of the *Stadttheatre Basel*.

Intendant: "Wenn Sie nicht einen so teuren Wagen fahren würden, wären Ihre Ausgaben geringer."

"I'm wondering if you weren't driving such an expensive car you would find it easier to make ends meet."

Paul: "Den Wagen habe ich in Kanada gekauft und er kostet mich nur den Treibstoff fur Benzin."

"I bought and paid for the car in Canada and the only thing it costs me is diesel fuel."

The conversation ended with no present agreement. One week later, Paul Frey left the theater smiling. "I got a new three-year contract with my raise!"

33

Settling In for the Long Run

REHEARSALS FOR *WERTHER* BEGAN once *Fidelio* opened. Paul carried fond memories of singing the role to Maureen Forrester's Charlotte in Stuart Hamilton's 1975 Opera in Concert at the St. Lawrence Hall in Toronto. It had been a turning point in his career.

Composed by Jules Massenet in 1892 and sung in French, Werther *the opera was based on the novel* The Sorrows of Young Werther. *It was written in 1892 by German writer Johann Wolfgang von Goethe.*

The poet hero Werther is in love with Charlotte, a young woman who is betrothed to Albert. Returning Werther's love, Charlotte still choses to honor her commitment to Albert and sends Werther away. Unable to exist in a world without his love, Werther kills himself with Alfred's pistol. On his deathbed, Charlotte confesses his love for him.

Paul calls Werther's aria "Why awaken me, O breath of spring" an aspiration of every operatic tenor.

> *Pourquoi me réveiller, ô souffle du printemps?*
> *Pourquoi me réveiller?*
> *Sur mon front, je sens tes caresses*
> *Et pourtant bien proche est le temps*
> *des orages et des tristesses!*

> Why awaken me, oh breath of spring?
> Why awaken me?
> on my brow, I feel your caresses,
> and yet, very close is the time
> of storms and sadness!

Settling In for the Long Run

Preparations for *Werther* saw Paul now working with Basel's head role coach, Rainer Altorfer. The professional relationship between the two would last until Paul's retirement. Paul had traveled a long distance, singing in the French language from his arduous preparations for *Faust* at the Summer Music Workshop in Waterloo. Still, French was a bugbear for him and he'd need to work diligently to bring his language skills up to the perfection he demanded of himself.

Altorfer, fluent in four languages—German, Italian, French, and English—was a fine match for this Canadian tenor. A perfectionist who saw diction and expression of words as essential to a great opera performance as the musical notes, Altorfer would find a keen pupil in Paul Frey.

"Paul's work ethic was outstanding," he reflected on his working relationship, which began more than forty years before with the Canadian tenor.[54] "He wanted to do things to the very best of his ability and was willing to work—work very hard to achieve them. And if it took him longer to find that perfection, he was willing to spend that time."

Unlike many singers who only practiced during their coaching sessions, Paul Frey did his homework on his own time. "And the result was usually impeccable," compliments Altorfer. And the voice! Altorfer calls the glorious sound that came from Paul Frey "bright and shiny without getting too white" ("white" meaning tinny). Rare among dramatic tenors, Altorfer adds: "His best notes were in the upper octave between G and B flat."

Rehearsals with the rest of the *Werther* cast commenced soon after the individual coaching. Now they were in the hands of the opera stage director. As is the case in live theater and film, opera directors are always looking for an original way to present. No easy task, given that the "old standards" have been performed hundreds of times over the decades. And so, striving for memorability, they may occasionally stray into the bizarre in their theatrical creativity. Such was the case with Basel's visiting stage director John Dew's 1979 production of *Werther*.[55]

Having performed the opera conventionally with Maureen Forrester in Toronto, Paul was surprised and dismayed by Dew's interpretation. "Dew's idea was that the action that takes place on stage was all a dream—Werther's dream. So Werther—that was me—had to be lying on stage 'dreaming' when he wasn't part of the action." It didn't take Paul Frey

Part 7: A New Life in Basel

too long to figure out that if he was on stage for the entire duration of the opera, he would have little opportunity to take a rest, quench his thirst, or use the facilities.

Still, he didn't feel at this early stage of his career that he could protest. "If a disagreement between a performer and the stage director occurs, the director will always win. Performers can always be replaced—there are 100 of them for every one stage director." As such, Paul Frey as Werther dreamed his way through each performance.

34

Some Constructive Criticism

HAVING MISSED HIS CLIENT's debut in *Fidelio*, Paul's agent, Ioan Holender, made the trip from Vienna to Basel to hear his *Werther*. And while Holender praised the performance, he had some words of caution too.

"Holender felt that I was overextending myself," recalls Paul of their conversation. "He pointed out that *Werther* is usually sung by a lyric tenor, one whose voice register is high and light. *Fidelio* is favored by dramatic tenors with a lower and more powerful voice register. And I was somewhere in the middle, able to sing both." Holender had concerns that by advertising this versatility, his client was becoming too much of a generalist. "Casting management wouldn't know what I was and that might be a disadvantage to me in the future in casting."

And as for his client performing in the operetta *A Night in Venice* and, even more outlandish, as the feature performer in a later operetta production devoted to the works of Italian composer Gaetano Donizetti and the French Charles Gounod, Holender was pleased even less! Paul disagreed with his agent. "I wanted to sing as often as I could—and I planned to."

Paul had later cause to revise his generalist mindset. In a September 24, 1987 interview with *Kitchener-Waterloo Record* writer Pauline Durichen, he stated: "I learned that versatility wasn't always good in opera due to the *Fach*." For her opera-challenged readers, Durichen explained *Fach* as: "that mysterious largely unwritten code of opera typecasting by which the character of singers' voices, not just raw power determines which chunk of standard works they should specialize in."[56]

To Durichen, Paul confessed: "No one had told me about *Fach* in Opera School—that is, not to mix Italian lyric with German Wagnerian."

And so, he confessed to the journalist, in his early Basel years he'd paid little attention to its importance. Paul later came to revise his early versatility. "Yes, I did everything well, but what was I? A lyric tenor? Or a heroic/heldentenor?"

Not all in the opera know would have agreed with agent Ion Holender. Another European opera agent sitting in the audience at the *Stadttheatre* had heard Paul Frey, in fine voice, sing *Werther*. Lyric *Fach* or dramatic *Fach* aside, this Canadian could sing! And what, the agent wondered, was he doing at a second-tier opera house such as Basel?

"This agent sought me out after the performance and told me that he felt that I should be singing in Paris. He offered to make a connection on my behalf." Paul was flattered and took the agent up on his offer. Arrangements were made and several weeks later, Paul Frey found himself in the historic *Palais Garnier*, home of Paris opera. "Nothing came of it," reports Paul. "It was far too soon in my career; I wasn't ready for Paris."

The Paris sojourn also allowed him the opportunity to meet his hero, Canadian tenor Jon Vickers. Vickers was starring in French composer Camille Saint-Saens's *Samson and Delilah*, and Paul made arrangements to visit the star in his dressing room. He recalls the brief, but illuminating meeting:

"I introduced myself, saying I was a Canadian tenor too. I told him that in the beginning of my career, I'd used his voice as a model for how I wanted mine to develop. In fact, I said, that many people who heard me compared my voice to his."

Never known for tact or graciousness, Vickers snorted: "Ridiculous! It's clear from your speaking voice that you're a lyric tenor, not a heroic tenor. Your voice is too high to sing heroic." "And that was about all there was to our meeting," reminisces Paul. "I left still thinking of him as my hero—at least as far as singing was concerned."

Paul returned to Basel having met Jon Vickers and knowing that he was not ready for the bright lights of Paris.

35

Time Zone Mayhem

PAUL HAD BEEN INVITED to sing Handel's *The Messiah* in Hamilton, Ontario over the Christmas holidays. He, Linda, and Ben had planned to return to Canada for Christmas anyway, and as his schedule didn't see him back in Basel performing until December 28, he felt the timing was good. Still, as an employee beholden to the *Stadttheatre Basel*, he'd need to ask permission. In a mood of goodwill, intendant Statkus agreed.

The family had settled comfortably into life in a cosmopolitan European city. They'd made social connections, primarily through Linda's membership in the American Women's Club. Canadian Thanksgiving saw the Freys inviting several families to share in a traditional Canadian meal of turkey and pumpkin pie. No mean feat considering the miniature size of Swiss refrigerators!

The majesty of the Swiss mountain backdrop invited the family to leave the city on weekends. Paul laughs: "We were used to the size of Canada compared to Switzerland, so we'd get in the car and before you knew it, we'd reached the border of Italy!"

Not that everything was perfect in beautiful, peaceful, and advanced Switzerland. And while Paul felt a kinship to the Swiss love of order, precision, and just "doing things right," the national temperament could go over the top. "I might be out cutting my lawn or working in my garden and a neighbor would stop to tell me I wasn't doing it right; I wasn't doing it *his* way. This was irritating for sure."

Part 7: A New Life in Basel

On the other hand, the Swiss reserve was welcome. "I rarely, if ever, had anyone at the stage door wanting a photo or my autograph. Even on the street, they might recognize me as a performer, but rarely would anyone ever stop me." He didn't appreciate the Swiss natural politeness fully until he experienced opera-rabid, "get in your face" Germany.

Before you could say "Swiss chocolate," it was holiday time and the Frey family were anticipating their return to Canada. Flying from London to Toronto was considerably less expensive than flying from Switzerland to Toronto, so the Freys decided to do a little European adventure before they boarded a plane.

"So we caught the train in Basel and that took us across the corner of Germany, through France to Calais. Then we got on the hovercraft to cross the English Channel. Finally, another train took us up to London." There the family boarded the flight to Toronto. Paul calls the itinerary "a bit of an ordeal" but notes that the cost savings were worth the effort. "And Ben loved the trip—trains and fast-boats especially."

Paul had booked their return journey (direct this time) to Basel on December 27. This would give him a day to adjust to the time change before he appeared on stage. It was not until bags were packed for the return visit that Paul pulled out the plane tickets. And he did a double take! Indeed, the flight to Switzerland left Toronto International Airport on the 27th, but it would be the afternoon of the 28th before it landed. "I wasn't enough of a seasoned traveler to account for the time difference between Canada and Europe," admits Paul. "It would be a tight fit," he recalls thinking. "I'd have to head straight to the theater after I landed. But I'd make it."

Meanwhile, as the sun rose on Basel the morning of December 28, the management of the *Stadttheatre* was worried. They'd not heard a peep from their star tenor, Mr. Paul Frey. No answer at the Frey home when they called by telephone either. The next step was to send a messenger to knock on the door. No answer!

By then, in turmoil, given there was no understudy for the always-reliable, never-ill Canadian, management went into crisis mode. They put out a call for a tenor who could sing the part. Paul recalls the scene when he arrived at the theater—with time to spare. "There was the stand-in singer ready to go on."

Time Zone Mayhem

Paul Frey hurriedly dressed and applied makeup and took his first cues. After the performance, he was buttonholed by Herr Statkus to cover the cost of hiring the stand-in. Taking a chance on his value to the theater, Paul held the line. "I was there on time; I sang the show, so I have no intention of paying for the replacement." Theater management was enamoured enough with their star tenor that they acquiesced.

Still, it was good lesson for future flying.

36

Three of Three

WITH *WERTHER* SAFELY LAUNCHED, rehearsals began for the third of Basel's three operatic productions for the season 1977–1978. It was Czech composer Bedrich Smetana's *The Bartered Bride*. Less performed than Beethoven's *Fidelio* or Massenet's *Werther*, the work is called a comic opera.

Composed between 1863 and 1866, the narrative takes place in a country village and follows the trail of true love prevailing, despite the meddling of parents and a marriage broker.

Smetana's opera borrows from traditional Czech culture in its musical score as well as dance—Bohemian polka and the rapidly-moving furiant. Written in Czech, Smetana's language, the opera is usually sung in German.

Joining Canadian Paul Frey in *The Bartered Bride* was American soprano Patricia Kadvan. With a voice described as having a "velvety smoothness . . . a dark and sultry timbre and remarkable breath control," Pat Kadvan would remain in Basel for only two or three years, before moving on to other opera houses. However, she would remain in contact with Paul over the years.[57]

As had been the case with *Fidelio* and *Werther*, Paul Frey's performance in *The Bartered Bride* was lauded. Theater management congratulated themselves for landing such a prize catch. And the 1977–1978 season at the *Stadttheatre Basel* wasn't quite over. "I still had *Night in Venice* (*Eine Nacht in Venedig*)," the ambitious tenor reports. Written by Johann Strauss II in three acts, the mood of the piece is romantic; the story line is farcical, revolving around mistaken identity. Not as strenuous or lengthy as the three operas, Paul was able to have fun with this last obligation.

With season one a success, Paul reflected on the reaction of theater management as well as his audiences to his performances. "I knew that management was pleased—after all, I'd been awarded a new contract and a raise in pay. And the positive press reviews told me that audiences liked what I was doing too." There were few autographs or requests for photos at the stage door though. These Swiss were a reserved bunch. That was just fine with the low-key Canadian.

With the theater going on summer hiatus, the Frey family prepared to return to Canada for July and August. Visiting family and friends was on the agenda. For Paul, the summer was an occasion to rest body and voice after a jam-packed first season. Three operas sung with two operettas thrown in for good measure. It had been a very rewarding—and promising—first year.

Paul Frey, age six

The Glad Tidings Quartet—Paul middle back with Cal Cressman, Ray Martin; seated Clare Bauman

The Schneider Male Quartet—Paul Frey bottom row, fourth left

Paul's home base, the *Stadttheatre Basel*

Frey home in Burg im Leimental, Switzerland

Frey family at home—
Ben, Linda, Paul

Florestan in *Fidelio*, Athens, Greece

Fencing instruction

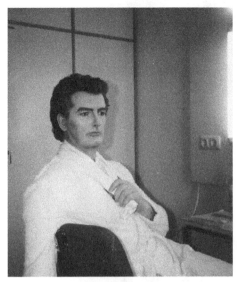

Paul Frey publicy shot, early 1980s

The makeup room

Star tenor Peter Hofmann; Paul replaces him in Wagner's *Lohengrin*

Paul Frey as Lohengrin—
Eva Johansson as Elsa

Paul Frey with Bayreuth *Festpielehaus* head Wolfgang Wagner

Bayreuth *Lohengrin* director Werner Herzog

Ben and Paul Frey in Bayreuth, Germany

Paul Frey in Werner Herzog's Bayreuth *Lohengrin*

In full-dress Lohengrin

Signing autographs in Bayreuth

La Bohème, Paris

Dr. Paul Frey D. Litt.,
Wilfrid Laurier University 2005

Part 8

Branching Out

(1979–1982)

37

Radio Gigs

PAUL DOVE INTO REHEARSALS for the first opera of his second year in Basel. It would be a full season, with four full-length works on the playbill. First up was *Tosca*, an opera in three acts by Italian composer Giacomo Puccini. Melodramatic in tone, *Tosca*'s plot is set in the Rome of the early 1800's. With Napoleon's army set to invade Italy, torture, murder, and suicide are the order of the day.

Mozart's *La Clemenza Di Tito*, set during the domination of the Roman Empire, would be the second work presented in Basel. Mozart's *Don Giovanni*, based on the life of the great lover Don Juan, would be followed by a repeat of Smetana's *The Bartered Bride*.

And if that wasn't enough enrichment, Paul's second year would also see him branching outside of the *Stadttheatre*. He'd be doing a bit of traveling. As late as the early 1980's, a number of radio stations broadcasting from midsize to large European cities presented musical programming, including opera and oratorio concerts. Each station also employed musicians and orchestra conductors. The larger the city, the larger the orchestra.

Stations in more metropolitan centers even boasted a theater where performances attended by the general public were staged. Radio Lugano in the city of Lugano, Switzerland was one. Paul had been approached by an American conductor living in Switzerland who led the Lugano radio orchestra. The man wished to produce the opera *Les Troyens* (*The Trojans*) for his radio program with Paul Frey singing the lead tenor role of Aeneas.

Based on Virgil's epic poem *The Aeneid*, *Les Troyens* was no easy gig.[58] At more than five hours in length, the score also calls for singer stamina. "It soars from the deeper baritone notes up to high C, so it's not an easy opera for the tenor voice," Paul states. Performed in French, *Les Troyens* surely brought back Paul's memories of his arduous experience learning the language for *Faust* at the Summer Music Workshop in Waterloo.

"My agent would have advised me not to do it, feeling at this early stage in my career that it was too big for me." But the invitation had come directly to Paul, not to Holender, and the singer had no thoughts of turning the challenge down. "So I agreed, happily." Paul worked diligently with voice coach Rainer Altorfer to master not only the complex score, but the French libretto.

Performing before a studio audience of around 600 people, Paul was happy with his performance and considered his radio debut a success. He'd surely agree to more if they came along. And they did. Over the next two years, radio listeners could tune in to Radio Lugano to hear his ringing tenor. Paul enjoyed the diversion and the extra money that the radio gig brought in was welcome.

With the knowledge that his job was secured for three years at least, the Freys were looking for a house to rent. Both country born and raised, Paul and Linda Frey were anxious to leave the city. Thanks to Rupert Forbes, Paul's Scottish friend in the opera company, they heard of a rental house in the village of Burg im Leimental, a half-hour out of Basel. Little could they have predicted that Burg would remain their home over the next twenty-five years. The extra room allowed them to accommodate friends and family from home. And so the Frey household became a convenient "hotel" for vacationing Canadians. "I remember once we had about sixteen Canadians staying with us," Paul laughs. It was surely the Frey Hotel.

38

Into Germany

Opera Houses like the *Stadttheatre Basel* hired two types of performers: contract or house singers like Paul Frey, who were paid a regular salary and owed their allegiance first to their employer, and freelance singers, who came in for a particular performance and were paid for such.

Illness of a house performer was one reason to bring in a freelancer. *Fach* was another. If, when Paul was offered the Basel contract, he had deferred doing either *Werther* or *Fidelio*, Horst Statkus would have been required to hire a guest tenor. They saved money when Paul offered to sing both. The star factor was also a consideration when bringing in guest performers. A Maria Callas, a Joan Sutherland, a Jon Vickers, or a Richard Tucker would bring out the press. And that was for what every performing venue strived.

But even with a weekly paycheck from a long-term contract, house performers were allowed to freelance. "As long as it didn't interfere with your primary employment, theater management usually supported it." Paul qualifies this: "In the theater's view they 'owned' their singers and they could say no to him or her taking a role elsewhere. But they better have a good reason for refusing it—and they usually didn't."

As guest performers arrived in Basel, many expressed admiration for its house tenor, Canadian Paul Frey. And invariably the conversation turned to what freelance work he was doing.

Guest: "You've got a great voice—adaptable too. I'm guessing you do a lot of freelancing outside Basel."

Paul: "Uh, no. I've only sung a couple of times on Radio Lugano."

Guest: "Why is that? I'd think that opera houses would be lining up to invite you in to sing."

Part 8: Branching Out

Paul: "I'd love to be doing more freelance work, but as I've only been here in Basel a couple of years, I guess not too many opera houses know about me.

Guest: Well, I doubt if that will last long. They'll hear about you sooner than later, I'll wager.

The wager was spot on. When the freelance floodgates opened, the water poured in. First was an invitation from Freiburg, Germany to sing Mendelsson's oratorio *Paulus* (*St. Paul*). A booking from the Montreal Symphony to sing Beethoven's *Ninth Symphony* oratorio followed on its heels. The opera world outside Basel was beginning to sit up and take notice, and with each freelance offer, Paul Frey's self-confidence grew. It was that same self-confidence that propelled him towards his first difference of opinion with intendent Statkus.

Basel wished to produce a work by French composer Jean-Philippe Rameau. Rameau wrote primarily for ballet but some of his operas caught the eye of opera houses too. Paul Frey read the score and libretto and was immediately dismayed on several counts. "The role called for me singing *coloratura*—that is trills, runs, and leaps in the musical score. I wasn't comfortable with this technique."

Secondly, the production would have him attached to a suspended wire allowing him to "fly" across the stage and above the audience. "And there was no way I was OK with that." So Paul refused to sing the part, suggesting that they bring in a guest artist on this occasion. His tenor's flat refusal to agree shocked intendent Statkus. "The Basel management was just so used to me doing everything that they asked. They couldn't believe that I refused to do it."

Negotiations between the two sides proceeded until there was a standoff. "It got to the point that Herr Stadkus communicated with me in writing." Paul held his ground. "And Stadkus finally gave up." Paul's self-assurance in his worth to the *Stadttheatre Basel* had been tested, and he'd won. A guest performer was brought in to sing the role and fly like a bird.

Another, more high-profile German engagement followed in the summer of 1981. A friend who sang in the Basel chorus was a Frey fan and gave Paul a valuable contact for the annual Eutin, Germany Opera Summer Fest. Eutin was the birthplace of famed German composer Carl Maria von Weber. The composer's most renowned opera, with spoken dialogue, is *Der Freischütz*, or *The Marksman*. Culturally important, as well as popular with audiences, von Weber's work is considered one of the earliest operatic examples of the celebration of the German cultural identity.

Into Germany

Paul auditioned for the role of Max the Forester in *Der Freischütz*. He won it and was off to the Opera Summer Fest. His memories are colorful, if not professionally satisfying. "The performances were all outdoors on the grass covering the grounds of a castle, with a natural hill employed as the stage. However, this summer happened to be an extremely wet one. The orchestra was covered with a makeshift roof but we performers were not. By the end, I was wearing rubber boots so I wouldn't slip on the wet grass."

Wet or dry, rubber boots or shoes, Paul's performance at this high-profile summer festival was an important step in his career. His first three-act operatic gig outside Basel was under his belt, and it had gone well. Very well indeed!

Paul's three-year contract ended in the summer of 1982. He felt confident that he'd be offered a two-year extension. His confidence received a boost when he heard, via the theater grapevine, about an audible comment that Armin Jordan, Basel's orchestra conductor, had made in the theater's canteen.

Jordan had the reputation as a tippler and one day, "in his cups," had offered his opinion, to anyone in earshot, of their star tenor—whose contract was coming up for renewal. "If there's one person we need to keep, it's Paul Frey," bellowed Herr Jordan. Paul chuckles: "So I figured I was in a good bargaining space with Herr Statkus when contract time came."

Conductor Jordan was not the only Basel administrator who was firmly in the Frey Admiration Society. Head stage director Martin Markun, recalling Paul's time in Basel, recalls him as "the ideal singer for a conductor or director."[59] Not only was the tenor's voice "impressive and touching," says Markun, "but as an actor he was sensitive and moving." Still, the Canadian's ambition shone through. "He always wanted a challenge," recalled Markun from his home in Basel.

It came as no surprise to the company that when Paul Frey left the intendant's office at the end of his third season, 1981, it was with the security of a new two-year contract.

39

Italian Adventure

By 1981, Paul was receiving regular oratorio invitations to perform in Germany. And for those gifts he was grateful. The Germans loved their classical music, and performance houses proliferated throughout the country. Paul was confident that invitations to sing opera would begin tricking in too. And they did. His first two calls were to replace ailing tenors in productions of *The Bartered Bride* in Wiesbaden, Germany and Mussorgsky's *Boris Godunov* in Bremen. It was a start.

Then came an invitation for a few members of the Basel company to perform the soundtrack for a movie production of Richard Wagner's last opera, *Parsifal*. It was being filmed in Monte Carlo, in the principality of Monaco. A field trip to some of Monte Carlo's famed casinos was *de rigueur* for many in the Basel company. But no gambling was done by the company's Canadian Mennonite!

An invitation from Genoa, Italy to sing the part of Alwa in Alban Berg's *Lulu* marked Paul's first invitation to take a full contract outside Basel. The role straddled the line between romantic lead and the less prestigious character tenor. Still, experience was experience, and Paul Frey was glad to embrace it. He'd not had the opportunity before of being part of a production with quite the notoriety as Lulu.

Written between 1929 and 1935 by Austrian composer Alban Berg, the opera centers on the beautiful and alluring Lulu. She's a seductive temptress who collects lovers as other women do jewelry. Once wearied of her conquests, she either murders them or drives them to suicide. Ultimately arrested for the murder of one lover, she is incarcerated. After her release from prison, Lulu

Italian Adventure

becomes a prostitute who meets her demise at the hands of a client as notorious as herself—Jack the Ripper.

Composer Berg died before the third act of his opera was completed, and for the next forty years it was performed incomplete. Even then *Lulu* attracted considerable attention. Labelled as "bourgeois", and banned in the Soviet Union, *Lulu* was decried as "degenerate" by Nazi Germany and was likewise *verboten*. Not until the death of Berg's widow in 1976 could steps be taken to complete the opera. Composer Friedrich Cerha took on the task. *Lulu* was first performed in its entirety in 1980 at the *Opera Germain* in Paris. The lead role was taken by Canadian soprano Teresa Stratas.

Written in German, *Lulu* had been translated into Italian for audiences in that country. As such, Paul took a course in Italian before taking up the role of Alwa, the Composer. Memorizing the libretto was only one part of performing his roles. Being able to communicate with support employees like stage director, stage hands, and wardrobe was essential for the conscientious Paul Frey.

It would be a two-hour drive from Basel to Genoa for three weeks of rehearsal and three weeks of the performance. But the ambitious Canadian was able to fit it into his Basel performance schedule. That was essential before any freelancing gigs. Still, there was one detail Paul needed to attend to before he headed south to Genoa.

"Italy had a terrible reputation for car theft," says Paul. "So there was no way I was going to drive my Mercedes and leave it parked while I was working." A friend was selling his old Audi for 700 francs, and Paul figured it was well worth the cost to buy the car and drive it back and forth to Genoa. Paul's plan worked only for a few days. "One day I came out and the car had been vandalized. The driver's side window had been smashed. Not to get anything inside, because I had left nothing. It was just vandalism."

Acclimatizing to the Italian, hence more relaxed concept of time, as opposed to the precise, orderly German-Swiss way, was an adjustment too. "8:00 could mean 8:20 or 8:35 in Genoa time," offers Paul. Then there was the preparedness factor. "In Genoa it wasn't unheard of to be handed props for the performance without ever having used them in rehearsal." Still, Genoa was valuable for Paul in his ongoing opera education.

Years later, when a long-held dream of singing at the great La Scala opera house in Milan was realized, Paul encountered the same *laissez-faire* attitude, both with respect to promptness and absence of props in rehearsals. "I much preferred the buttoned-down Swiss way," he advises.

Part 8: Branching Out

Paul's fifth season in Basel also saw the realization of a dream he'd carried since Opera School. That was the chance to explore the deep waters of German composer Richard Wagner. The memories of the initial time he had heard the divine Wagner came flooding back to him when he learned that Basel would be producing the composer's *Der Fliegende Hollander* (*The Flying Dutchman*).

"I heard Wagner's *Hollander* for the first time when I was in Toronto, singing in the chorus of the Canadian Opera Company, who were producing it. When the chorus wasn't needed on stage, we hung out in the green room, playing cards or relaxing. But when I heard Wagner's music I was so mesmerized that I stood quietly behind the stage curtain just so I could listen to it."

Now Paul would have his own chance with Wagner. He'd be singing the lead tenor role of Erik the Hunter in Basel's production of *Der Fliegende Hollander*. Admitting that his knowledge of the great Wagner, at the time, was minimal, he only knew in his heart that the music resonated deeply with him.

He'd come to know Wagner even more in the coming months of his blossoming operatic career.

Part 9

Next Five Years—Basel? Or Elsewhere?

(1982–1985)

40

Tenure for Life?

By the summer of 1982, Paul Frey's life was unfolding as it should. "I'd always liked to think in five-year terms," he explains. "It was five years from Opera School to Basel; now it was five years in Basel. And I'd see what came next over the next five years."

He'd built up an impressive list of operatic credits to his name, singing in three languages. In German: *The Bartered Bride, Fidelio, Makropulos, Der Fliegende Hollander, Boris Gudunov, Electra, Ariadne aux Naxos,* and *Der Freischütz.* In Italian, he'd sung: *Don Giovanni, La Bohème, Macbeth, Rigoletto, Tosca, Il Tabbaro, La Clemenza de Tito,* and *Lulu.* And in French: *Werther* and *Les Troyens.*

Thus far into his professional career, Beethoven's *Fidelio* stood high on his list of favorites. "The plot lines of so many of the operas were silly, fantastical, lightweight. But *Fidelio* was a story with the important themes of freedom, justice, determination, and love. Every time I sang *Fidelio* I felt I put more into it than the previous time. I felt that I'd done something worthwhile."

A meeting with Johann Strauss's *Electra* provided no such fond feelings. Based on Greek mythology, Strauss's work focusses on the heroine Electra's emotions. Murder, blood, and gore predominate—themes made more vivid with Basel's performance, which was set in a slaughterhouse.

And so for Paul Frey, the logical next step in his career was negotiating another five-year deal in Basel. "That would give me tenure for life," he explains. It was security that few in the operatic world had.

The family had settled comfortably into life in the small municipality of Burg im Leimental (Le Bourg in French), just outside Basel, close to the French border. Burg's most famous citizen was Swiss scientist Albert

Part 9: Next Five Years—Basel? Or Elsewhere

Hofmann, the first scientist to synthesize lysergic acid diethylamide, or LSD. Primarily forested, with some agricultural land, Burg had welcomed Paul, Linda, and Ben Frey. Comfortable in their charming rental home, when the opportunity came to purchase the property and house, the Freys had no hesitation. Eventually they would add an extension, primarily to offer accommodation for the many Canadian friends and relatives who visited. They'd developed a circle of Basel friends as well.

On the other hand, there was a whole other opera world far beyond the majestic Alps to explore for Paul Frey. And he was driven to explore it. He'd sampled bits and pieces of that allure during freelance contracts, and he sought more. "If I went freelance instead of locking myself into another five-year contract, I'd be available to take up more offers," Paul reasoned. And those offers were coming in with regularity now.

In the battle between "stay" and "go," it was caution that won the day. Paul agreed to a new five-year deal to begin his sixth season in Basel. He'd be building his repertoire with Wagner and Haydn's less well-known *Orlando Paladino*, a tale of unrequited love, madness, and a magician named Zoroastro.

Vocal coach Rainer Altorfer, who worked closely with Paul before all his Basel performances, has memories of his star pupil's attitude in learning each new role. "I noticed from the first time we worked together that Paul cared a lot about good diction—how the words were pronounced. In fact, in comparing him to other singers—some considered 'greater' than him—he stood out in the front. Paul was always precise."[60]

As for the Canadian's stylistic interpretations of the music? Altorfer remembered them as "impeccable." It was these attributes, added to his work ethic, that would, the coach predicted, allow Paul to rise rapidly in the opera world.

The third opera on the Basel schedule was Richard Wagner's *Tannhäuser*. Paul was taking a pass on this monster and a guest artist would be brought in. Historically, the music had proved too vocally challenging and exhausting for most tenors to take on and Paul had no wish to prove them wrong. "*Tannhäuser* is perhaps the most difficult of Wagner's operas," he explains. "It's just too big, too strenuous, with notes that soar from low to high. It was known as a 'voice-wrecker,' and I had no plans to sing it."

Paul adds that he was in good company in this choice. "Most of the top tenors such as Placido Domingo and Jon Vickers refused to sing *Tannhäuser* live," he states. "Domingo sang it for a recording but that was

Tenure for Life?

far different than live on a stage." And when the role was performed live, it wasn't unknown to have two singers do the part: one to sing the first half, another for the second half.

For the Basel production, an American guest artist performed the role—accomplishing the monolith "quite well," reports Paul Frey.

Invitations were now coming from outside the German-Austrian-Swiss opera stronghold. Paul had been offered his first full opera contract as "second cast," in Madrid. Paul explains the "first cast, second cast" practice.

"The two large Spanish opera houses, Madrid and Barcelona, operated differently than the German-speaking ones. Opera in Spain went by the *stagioni* system, which meant that they only staged operas a few times over the season. They then hired singers and orchestra to perform on short-term contracts. When the performance ended, the opera stage remained dark until next time."

Sometimes "first cast" performers couldn't commit to an entire run (or the theater could only afford a big name for one or two productions). In these cases, a "second cast" would step in to finish the run.

When a call came to Paul Frey from Madrid to be second cast for the tenor lead role of Erik the Hunter in *Der Fliegende Holländer*, and it fit into his Basel commitment schedule, Paul accepted. It was an eye-opener to opera elitism.

"Most of the singers I worked with in Madrid were from higher-ranked German and Austrian houses—Munich, Hamburg, Vienna. When I arrived, they asked me where I was from and I answered Basel. They actually snubbed me! Basel was considered well down on the prestige level of opera houses." Paul adds, with satisfaction, that as soon as they heard his voice, the snobbery was discontinued.

During the early 1980's, Paul also performed a number of *Messiah* oratorios in Canada: in Edmonton, Winnipeg, and Toronto. Then there was Paul Frey in *The Student Prince* in his hometown of Kitchener-Waterloo, Ontario. Starring in Sigmund Romberg's oft-performed operetta was a particularly meaningful one for him. "Mario Lanza singing *The Student Prince* was the first classical music I had ever heard. It was because of this that I decided to study opera." The Kitchener appearance also included some out-of-concert-hall fun. Paul waved to crowds from a convertible as he rode in the annual mammoth Oktoberfest parade.

Part 9: Next Five Years—Basel? Or Elsewhere

Although North American bookings were in the minority, Paul wanted to keep this avenue open. "At this point, I still saw us at some time returning to Canada and continuing my career from there." So Paul felt it might be to his advantage to have a North American agent. He'd asked his Opera School mentor Louis Quilico for his recommendations and Quilico suggested Columbia Artists Management in New York City. Quilico would even make the connection, although Paul would need to do an audition.

Appearing in *Carmen* in Victoria, British Columbia, Paul decided to do a New York stopover before he headed back to Basel. Ushered into Columbia Artists Management agent Alan Green's office, Paul gave the man a sampling of his repertoire. We'll listen in on the conversation.

Agent Green: *"That's fine; you have a strong voice. And where are you employed now?"*

Paul: *"At the opera house in Basel. I've been there for several years, although I've been starting to do some freelance work in Germany, Spain, and Canada."*

Agent Green: *"Basel. That's in Switzerland? A small house, right?"*

Paul: *"I'd call it a second-tier opera house—medium size, according to European standards."*

Agent Green: *"Hmmmmm. Basel's a good place for you, right now. Yes, a good place."*

Paul left Columbia Artists Management embarrassed, angry, and with no offer to represent him. "Manager, management company," he muttered. "I'll do the work myself." His mood only lightened when his plane touched down on friendly Swiss soil.

41

A Shock Becomes a Blessing

CALLED INTO HERR STATKUS's office early in the fall of 1984, as he was beginning his seventh season in Basel, Paul was taken off guard by some unexpected news. The theater would be bringing a second-cast tenor, American Eduardo Villa, into the family. This would be Villa's first contract. Born in Los Angeles, he started his musical training as a violinist, later moving into musical comedy as a student at Santa Barbara City College in Los Angeles.

Villa eventually found his true *métier* in opera and studied at the University of Southern California. In 1982 he'd won the Metropolitan Opera auditions. Basel would be his first professional operatic contract as second cast to Paul Frey.

Not that Basel was the slightest bit disenchanted with Paul Frey, their number one tenor, Stadkus stressed. "But the administration had decided that my voice was better suited to the German operas than the Italian repertoire," recalls Paul. He would continue to take the lead roles in those productions. Villa's voice, management felt, was more suited to sing the Italian repertoire. And so, the American would sing those. They'd break him in with the Italian opera *Simon Boccanegra*, the first production of the season. Paul would take the first three performances; Villa the rest.

In his offer, Statkus, fully aware of Paul Frey's growing star power, was surely acting altruistically. "He suggested that given how much in demand I had become, the respite would allow me to take more freelance contracts. And my salary from Basel would stay the same."

Initially rattled, even feeling slighted at the time, Paul soon came to see and appreciate Statkus's offer. Still, there were certain drawbacks to the plan. "I wondered how becoming a German opera specialist would affect

Part 9: Next Five Years—Basel? Or Elsewhere

my marketability. At this point, I saw my future back in North America—Canada and hopefully the U.S. There, significantly more Italian and French operas were staged than German onoes. So I wanted to continue to build that repertoire. It just made me more marketable when I moved home."

And there was more uncertainty. While he enjoyed signing German opera—Strauss, Beethoven, von Weber—he'd even dipped his toe into Richard Wagner waters—this tenor was uncertain if German opera was in his best interests. Some time would be needed to sort this out.

In the meantime, he'd go out of Italian opera in Basel with a bang. As he worked with Rainer Altorfer preparing for *Simon Boccanegra*, Verdi's tale of intrigue, scandal, and pirates, he tried to make his voice caress both the score and the libretto. "I wanted to show the Basel people that I could do a great job on Italian opera too!"

His work ethic would pay it forward within a year.

The uncertain feelings that the Eduardo Villa situation had initially aroused were soon tempered by Paul's ever-increasing number of freelance offers. He'd developed a reputation as capable, reliable, last-minute fill-in for ailing tenors. Always prepared, always prompt, with no diva theatrics, Paul Frey was carving out for himself a niche, not only of talent but dependability. Growing up and pulling your weight in a farm family had its rewards—even in the opera world!

And then there were the mushrooming full-contract offers. Early fall 1985 saw his first invitation to perform a full opera in Germany. He'd done fill-in work in the opera-mad country before, but this was the real thing. The fact that the opera was *Fidelio*—at the top of his most-favored roles list—was a bonus. But it was the location, Heidelberg, which Paul felt was portentous.

"I'd been born in Heidelberg, Ontario; Heidelberg, Germany was the setting of *The Student Prince*, which I was listening to when I decided to follow an opera career. And now I was singing opera in Heidelberg, Germany. It just all seemed a good omen to me." He eagerly accepted the invitation and rented an apartment for the duration of rehearsals and performance—hoping to get home to visit his family as often as he could.

It wasn't long into the production that Paul's intuition about stars on his horizon grew brighter. One evening he was approached by an agent bearing compliments. Paul explains that European opera agents are expected to be all-knowing, always aware of which opera houses were staging

A Shock Becomes a Blessing

what opera and when. When they could put a singer—any singer—together with an opera house—any opera house—it was business for them.

We'll eavesdrop on their conversation—one that would ultimately change the course of Paul Frey's life.

Agent: *"Ich denke, Sie haben die perfekte Stimme für* Lohengrin. *Sie haben die Stärke im untern Register, aber Sie erhalten auch die höheren Töne. Haben Sie die Rolle gelernt?"*

"I think you have the perfect voice for Lohengrin. *You've got the power in the lower register but can get to the high notes too. Have you learned the role?"*

Paul: *"Noch nicht. Ich hatte es noch nicht gebraucht. Vielleicht sollte ich es."*

"Not yet I haven't. I haven't had the need to. Maybe I should."

Agent: *"Ich würde gerne ein Vorsingen in Karlsruhe für Sie arrangieren. Lassen Sie mich wissen, wenn Sie bereit sind und ich werde anrufen."*

"I'd be glad to arrange an audition in Karlsruhe for you. Let me know when you are ready and I'll make the call."

Paul: *"Das wäre toll. Vielen Dank."*

"That would be great. Thanks so much."

Over the coming days, between *Fidelio* performances in Heidelberg, Paul familiarized himself with the story of Richard Wagner's *Lohengrin*. The opera was set in the mythic northern land of Brabant in the eleventh century. The hero of Wagner's tale, Lohengrin, a Knight of the Holy Grail, arrives in the troubled land in a boat pulled by a swan. His holy mission is to save the life of a maiden condemned to death. In return, the maiden must never ask the knight's name.

Lohengrin struck a particular chord with Paul. The story—of fairness, justice, and good over evil—spoke to his inner values. Little could Paul Frey have imagined how the tale of the Swan Knight would alter the trajectory of his professional life.

42

A Perfect Match

Returning to Basel after *Fidelio*, Paul scheduled extra time with vocal coach Rainer Altorfer. They'd work together to prepare Paul for the *Lohengrin* audition that he hoped would come. Wagner's tale of the knight who travels in a boat pulled by a swan was in the planning stages for the busy Karlsruhe Opera Theatre.

The pair focused their attention on arias from the third act of the opera. Paul found the experience rewarding—and exhilarating. Somewhat to his surprise, he realized that Wagner's opera was a natural for him. "It just suited my voice; I was very comfortable singing it, right from the beginning."

Over thirty years later, coach Altorfer recalls Paul Frey learning Richard Wagner's *Lohengrin*. "We met a number of times, preparing for the audition. I was at the grand piano; Paul was singing in front of me. As always, he worked hard and very attentively. But one thing was clear from the beginning—how much the music suited him and he suited the music."

It appears that they had an audience enjoying the music too. Altorfer recalls: "There was a large window right behind us. One day we detected a movement on the window sill and we realized that it was a dove just sitting on the ledge outside. Maybe the bird could hear us and liked the sound, because it stayed—all through the preparations for the audition." Coach and singer began calling their feathered visitor "Lohengrin." "We felt the bird was good luck."

With Altorfer's expert guidance, Paul burned the midnight oil, perfecting both score and libretto. He felt confident that this would give the Karlsruhe people sufficient scope to judge his abilities—when the invitation came.

A Perfect Match

True to his word, Paul's agent guardian angel contacted him, indicating an audition had been set up. He needed only to get to Karlsruhe at the appointed time. As he boarded the train to Karlsruhe, a two-hour journey from Basel, Paul recalls his mood. "I was confident and calm; I had a really good feeling about what was going to happen."

Ushered into the Karlsruhe theater, Paul took his place beside the piano accompanist. He experienced a momentary flashback to a similar situation six years before on the Canada Council audition tour. "It was just me on a stage, beside a piano accompanist, singing for people I couldn't see, who were seated in a darkened audience." And while the setting and personnel were similar, the self-confidence of the singer was now far greater. "I sang well and waited for what I expected would be a favorable response." Out of the darkness came:

Them: *"'Höchste Vertrauen', haben sie nicht, oder?"*
"You don't have the 'Highest Confidence' do you?"
Paul: *"Wie bitte?"*
"Pardon me?"

"I was shocked and speechless," Paul recalls. "I thought I'd sung very well and with confidence." Sensing the singer's confusion, the next words from the darkened abyss were a relief:

Them: *"Ja, Ja, diesen teil aus dem dritten Akt, 'Höchste Vertrauen,' haben Sie noch nicht gelernt oder?"*
"Yes, but the passage in the third act, 'The Highest Confidence,' you haven't learned that yet, have you?"
Paul: *"Nein, habe ich nicht . . ."*
"No, I haven't . . ."
Them: *"Bitte gehen Sie noch Hause und lernen Sie diesen teil aus dem dritten Akt und kommen Sie zuruck bereit es zu singen."*
"Well go home and learn the selection in the third act and come back prepared to sing it."

With considerable relief and anticipation, Paul caught the train home to Basel. Over the next week he and coach Altorfer toiled to perfect the selection. Then it was back to Karlsruhe and part two of his audition. "I hit all the notes perfectly and was enjoying myself so much that I could have sung it twice." Still, he couldn't help but note a certain irony in the situation.

"*Lohengrin* is the most Italian of Wagner's German operas, and I was convinced that the work I did in Basel, learning *Simon Boccanegra*,

Part 9: Next Five Years—Basel? Or Elsewhere

proving that I could sing Italian opera with the best of them, got me the job in Karlsruhe."

No need for Karlsruhe to hear more. Paul was hired as second cast for *Lohengrin* in their upcoming production. East German tenor Klaus König was first cast. König would sing the first three performances; the company would then break for the summer. Then *Lohengrin* would resume in the fall with a new star: Paul Frey. It was uncertain how long *Lohengrin* would run. Demand would determine this.

But, Paul was next informed that only one tenor would be attending the six-week rehearsals. He explains this operatic "skipping school." "König had previously sung the role, so there was no need for him to spend all six weeks in rehearsals. He'd need to only brush up in a few rehearsals before opening night. So, the stage was mine." "To grow and learn," he might have added. That suited him just fine.

Returning to Basel after the audition, Paul's first stop was intendant Statkus. He asked to be released from his contract at the conclusion of the 1985–1986 season. "Herr Stadkus took it well; perhaps he wasn't that surprised because he was aware that I was doing a lot of contract work. He wished me good luck and hoped that I would come back as a guest performer from time to time."

And so Paul's five-year plan continued on schedule. He was setting out on a new journey, one that seemed to point him to Wagnerian opera. It rivaled the adventure he'd embarked on from Canada in 1977.

Part 10

Richard Wagner and Beyond

(1985–1986)

43

A Condensed Wagner Primer

As COMPLEX AND MULTIFACETED as his operas, Richard Wagner was surely a tormented genius. A look into his life brings some insight into the great operas he created—between the years 1842 and 1882.[61]

Birth records show that Wilhelm Richard Wagner was born in Leipzig, Germany on May 22, 1813. His mother is recorded as Johanna Rosine and his father as Carl Friedrich Wagner, a police actuary.

Recently, these documents have come under scrutiny. It is now believed that Wagner inherited his artistic genes from his true biological father, Ludwig Geyer, an accomplished painter, actor, and poet.

From an early age, young Richard was interested in the arts and wrote his first play, a five-act tragedy, Leubald und Adelaide, when he was still in grade school.

Music also inspired him and he took lessons in harmony and counterpoint. Leipzig, a significant cultural center, offered much to the precocious lad and he often attended musical performances in the city and beyond. Carl Maria von Weber's opera Der Freischütz and Beethoven's Fidelio particularly inspired him.

At age sixteen, he began composing seriously and enrolled at Leipzig University to study musical composition. So impressed was Wagner's music teacher that he had his student's composition Opus 1 published. Before he was twenty, Wagner made his debut as a conductor, with the orchestra performing his own Symphony in C Major.

Opera continued to inspire the young Wagner. From his earliest compositions, and rare among composers, Wagner wrote both the score and the libretto. His early love of literature influenced this practice.

Part 10: Richard Wagner and Beyond

Between 1833 and 1836, he composed his first opera, Die Feen *(The Fairies), but failed to get the work produced. His second opera,* Das Liebesverbot *(The Ban on Love), was based on William Shakespeare's* Measure for Measure. *It was the first of his works produced. Rife with political comments and criticisms,* Das Liebesverbot *was unpopular and closed after only one performance. The fiasco left the young composer bankrupt—a frequent situation over the extravagant Wagner's life.*

Marriage and Troubles Deepen

In 1836 Wagner married actress Minna Planer. Over the next year, the couple moved from town to town, seeking employment—Minna as an actress, Richard as the musical director—at one or another of the little theater companies that proliferated throughout Germany of the day.

In 1838, Wagner was appointed the musical director of the opera house in Riga, Latvia, on the Baltic coast, and the couple moved to this northern location. In his time away from the theater, Wagner began working on a new opera, Rienzi, der Letzte der Tribunen *(Rienzi, the Last of the Tribunes). This five-act tale, set in ancient Rome, sees the populist hero Rienzi outwitting the Roman nobles.*

He also began composition of Der Fliegende Hollander *(The Flying Dutchman), a tale revolving around the legend of a ship's captain doomed to sea forever.*

But Wagner's profligate ways soon saw him again in financial distress. With creditors at their heels, Richard and Minna picked up stakes and in the dead of night left Riga for Paris. In this grand opera capital, Wagner hoped to sell his latest compositions. The journey through the Baltic from Riga was a storm-tossed one—a situation that Wagner used to his benefit as he worked on Der Fliegende Hollander.

Arriving in Paris full of hope, the couple struggled over the next three years. Wagner was unable to find a buyer for his works. His left-leaning, antinobility themes were too revolutionary for the conservative Paris opera world. For a time, he and Minna lived hand to mouth with a rag-tag colony of German artists.

But rejection failed to dampen Wagner's creative spirit and he continued to write. In 1841 fortune finally smiled when the King of Saxony accepted Rienzi *for a production at the Dresden Court Theater.*

A Condensed Wagner Primer

Before he left Paris to return to Germany, Wagner began sketches for the opera that would eventually become his great work Tannhäuser.

Return to Germany

Much to Wagner's relief and joy, Rienzi was received warmly in Dresden. Audiences were dazzled by the stamina needed by its principal singers in enduring the opera's five-hour presentation. Wagner's fortunes also received a boost when he was appointed conductor of the court opera.

Der Fliegende Hollander, staged in 1843, received no such warm greeting from Dresden audiences. Expecting a conventional opera with arias showcased dramatically outside the story line, Wagner's production integrated the music with the narrative. Audiences were taken aback by this "integrated" approach. They complained loudly that they never knew when to applaud and when to sit on their collective hands. Audiences, it appears, were also disturbed by Hollander's dark mood and ghostly characters.

Undaunted, Wagner continued to create. He completed Tannhäuser and began the prose of Lohengrin, a medieval Germanic romance set in the mythical kingdom of Brabant. Both works reflected Wagner's growing fascination with ancient Germanic myths and legends. From this point on, mythology would permeate all of Wagner's works.

Financial Troubles Become Political

Tannhäuser was staged in Dresden in 1845. A sensual tale of love and lust set in the realm of Venus, Wagner's opera was initially coolly received by audiences and panned by critics. Slowly it gained supporters.

Over the next three years Wagner would finish Lohengrin and make plans for its staging. But as was seemingly the case, as soon as Wagner gained success, his demons worked to destroy the good. The composer's spendthrift ways and his increasing demands for artistic control of his productions were winning him no fans in court administration.

Wagner's visions now saw his musical productions, including opera, removed from court control, to be replaced with a national theater under his own jurisdiction. These revolutionary notions were anathema to the cultural powers that be, and even those who had supported Wagner's return to Dresden were now alienated. So potent was the dispute that the city of Dresden refused to allow the staging of Lohengrin, now complete.

Part 10: Richard Wagner and Beyond

Wagner's politics were increasingly strident. Now aligning himself with those who advocated revolution, Wagner took part in the plans for the Dresden uprising of 1849. A warrant was put out for his arrest and Wagner fled Germany for Zurich, Switzerland. In the composer's absence, Lohengrin *was presented in 1850, in Munich, by composer Franz Liszt.*

Exile

Over the next fifteen years, with Wagner in exile, none of his operatic works were presented. But the composer's creative spirit was far from fallow. A number of treatises advocating full-scale political and social revolution emerged from this period of his life. Hand in hand with these came artistic revolution.

Espousing a new egalitarian spirit, Richard Wagner decreed that his operas would no longer be enjoyed only by the elite of society. They were "for the people." Indeed, even the word "opera" was outlawed in Wagner's new artistic world. His productions were "music dramas."

Wagner's exile saw continuing compositional work. Now immersed in Norse legend, he began the creation of the Siegfried hero character, one who would emerge after the coming revolution. Out of this "new man" theme came the early stages of what would become his most ambitious work, Der Ring des Nibelungen.

Ultimately Der Ring *would be divided into four musical dramas:* Das Rheingold *(The Rhine Gold) as prelude,* Die Walküre *(The Valkyrie),* Siegfried, *and* Götterdämmerung *(The Twilight of the Gods) as the body of the grand work. Wagner envisioned* Der Ring *being presented over four closely spaced performances. He also began sketches for a new work based on the ancient Celtic romance* Tristan und Isolde.

It is during this time period that Wagner began a love affair with Mathilde Wesendonk, the wife of a rich patron. Such was the scandal that Wagner was, once again, forced to flee. This time he decamped to Venice, Italy and then Lucerne, Switzerland. In Lucerne he completed Tristan.

Return to Germany

In 1861 an amnesty allowed Wagner to return to Germany. There was little solace here. Opera companies refused to stage Tristan, *finding Wagner's innovations incomprehensible. In frustration (as much to put food on his threadbare*

A Condensed Wagner Primer

table as anything) he conceded to write a "normal" work. The result was Die Meistersinger von Nürnberg (The Mastersingers of Nuremberg).

Old habits die hard, and by 1864 Wagner was borrowing money from friends and associates, taking from Peter to stave off Paul. With debtor's prison a surety, once again Wagner fled.

At this point, much-needed serendipity knocked on Richard Wagner's battered door. King Ludwig II of Bavaria, only eighteen, ascended to the throne in 1864. A great admirer of Wagner's work, Ludwig settled all the composer's debts and gave him financial security to complete Der Ring in Munich.

Over the next six years, the king (smitten by the composer) facilitated productions of Wagner's previous works: Tristan und Isolde, Die Meistersinger, Das Rhinegold, and Die Walküre.

No sooner had good times come to call than Wagner's fatal flaws awakened. Flush with his recent successes, he spent lavishly and reawakened his political diatribes. And as if these excesses were not enough to turn the public against him, he'd begun an affair with Cosima, the wife of theater conductor Hans van Bulow and daughter of Wagner's great friend and composer Franz Liszt.

Despite King Ludwig's support, the ensuing scandal forced Wagner (and Cosima) to flee Munich, this time to Triebschen on Lake Lucerne in Switzerland. There they continued to enjoy the financial support of the benevolent king.

Cosima, more than twenty years Wagner's junior, bore him three children before she divorced van Bulow. The couple married in 1870.

The Bayreuther Festspielhaus

Wagner had become convinced that his works should be presented in a theater of his own design and construction. He'd found the ideal property to build his Festspielhaus (opera house) in the Bavarian town of Bayreuth. Now Wagner set out to raise the money to build it. His benefactor, King Ludwig, contributed generously to the theater and in 1872 enough funds had been collected to lay the foundation stones.

Ludwig also financed Wagner's lavish house, Wahnfried ("Peace from Illusion"), on the theater grounds. From there, the master could supervise all aspects of his theater.

By 1876, construction on the Festspielhaus was complete. Der Ring was presented over four performances. Audience response was uniformly enthusiastic.

Part 10: Richard Wagner and Beyond

Parsifal, *Wagner's last work, a tale of Arthurian knights and their search for the Holy Grail, was completed and performed in Bayreuth in 1882. Wagner had tailored the music to suit the sound of his magnificent theater.*

Richard Wagner's tumultuous life ended in 1883. Heart failure was the cause. Before his death he'd dictated his life story, Mein Leben *(My Life) to his wife, Cosima. He was buried in a tomb of his own design on the grounds of Wahnfried.*

44

Lohengrin, Karlsruhe

IN LATE AUGUST 1985, Paul returned to Karlsruhe to take his place as Lohengrin. Whether he'd continue to share the role with first-cast tenor Klaus König or take it over himself would become clear over the coming weeks. Fingers crossed. Given his reduced responsibilities at Basel, thanks to the hiring of Eduardo Villa, he hoped for the latter. No matter. He'd look to the present—opening night—and see what transpired.

From the moment Paul Frey as Lohengrin, Richard Wagner's Knight of the Holy Grail, glided onto the stage, in a boat pulled by a swan, he had the sold-out Karlsruhe audience in the palm of his hand. Over the ensuing five hours, with ease and with confidence, he became a star.

And there was more—much more—to come. Nothing that Canadian Paul Frey had experienced in opera before prepared him for the reception he received from those opening-night Karlsruhe audiences.

"There was standing ovation after standing ovation," he recalls, shaking his head at the memory. "And the protocol was that as long as the audience kept clapping, you continued to come out for curtain calls—no matter if there were two or fifty people clapping." And then there were the bouquets of flowers and gifts thrown onto the stage. The adulation continued in the hallways outside Paul's dressing room. "A crowd of people, wanting an autograph, wanting to talk to me, to give me flowers. It was overwhelming."

Nor did the frenzy abate after opening night. "The second, the third, the fourth, the fifth performances were pretty well the same," Paul remembers, with a note of incredulity. "I'd recognize some of the autograph seekers and say: 'Hey, didn't I give you an autograph last time?' No matter; there they were again, wanting another." Exhausted after a grueling performance,

Part 10: Richard Wagner and Beyond

Paul wanted nothing better than to divest himself of his character's costume and heavy makeup. Instead, his inborn Canadian politeness prevailed.

He'd begun to recognize the regulars. One elderly lady—"she reminded me of my mother"—appeared at every performance. "I learned that she didn't live in Karlsruhe but took the train whenever I sang." As Paul's fame and itinerary grew, and he performed across Europe, he could always count on his number-one fan. "She didn't fly but would take the train, even if my performance was in another country."

Paul would find himself on the receiving end of numerous gifts from adoring fans—scarves, gloves, even paintings. A gift too appeared in the person of one Rudolph Bautz, a voice coach. He'd been recommended by a colleague as a valuable resource in voice readiness, able to coax an operatic voice into a fit state for singing a five-hour Wagnerian opera.

Paul met with Bautz, and the two hit it off. Bautz found himself employed during the duration of the Karlsruhe engagement and beyond. Over the next ten years, Rudolph Bautz would accompany Paul on many of his European engagements. "I appreciated Rudolph's technical abilities as well as his positive compliments on my voice and my performances." Ironically, down the road, it would be Bautz's exuberance that would end the professional relationship between the opera tenor and the voice coach.

45

Somebody Important in the Audience

UNBEKNOWNST TO PAUL, DURING his third Karlsruhe performance a man bearing an extraordinary gift—one that would open the door to eventual worldwide opera fame—was in the audience. His name was Werner Herzog, and he was a veritable star in his own right.

Called "one of the prime architects" of the New German cinema of the 1970's, and the creator of such acclaimed films as *Aguirre the Wrath of God* and *Nosterafu*, Werner Herzog had been sent to Karlsruhe on a non-cinematic mission. On behalf of Wolfgang Wagner, director of the *Bayreuther Festspielhaus*, Herzog was wearing a talent scout hat rather than his usual director's *chapeau*.

Herzog had been contracted by Wagner to direct a new production of *Lohengrin* to debut at the 1987 edition of the annual summer festival, the *Festspiele*. A relative opera novice, Herzog had previously directed only Busoni's *Doktor Faust* in Bologna, Italy. But Bayreuth's top man was seeking a new look for Wagner's tale of a Knight of the Holy Grail who travels in a boat pulled by swan and arrives at a troubled kingdom to defend the honor of a princess. And he'd tagged the creative genius of Herzog to make it happen.

Wagner also wanted a new Lohengrin for that summer's *Festspiele* signature production. The buzz along the opera pipeline was that there was a promising tenor, a Canadian named Paul Frey, who'd been wowing audiences in Karlsruhe. He might be just the face and the voice that Wagner was looking for.

And so Wagner had dispatched Herzog to take a field trip to see for himself. The director arrived unannounced and unknown to the leading

Part 10: Richard Wagner and Beyond

man, to take his seat for the night's production. Thirty years after the fact, Herzog's memories of his first glimpse of Paul Frey as Lohengrin are dramatic and crystal clear. From his home in Los Angeles, he recalled.[62]

"Lohengrin first appears from the back of the stage. He's supposedly being pulled up the river in a boat by a swan. But just as the boat moved to the front of the stage, the set—at least fifteen feet of it—collapsed behind Paul. It was just like a tunnel collapsing into itself. Everyone in the audience, including me, gasped."

Herzog, clearly with a love of the dramatic, continues the tale: "And do you know what Paul Frey did? Do you know how he reacted as the entire set fell behind him? Nothing. He carried on as if nothing had happened—he sang his piece and moved into place. And he remained unfazed." Herzog adds: "But there was no way he couldn't have known what was going on behind him."

Paul Frey's memories of the scenery malfunction corroborate and clarify Herzog's. "I was actually on a platform that had been built to rest on a forklift, which was raised about twenty feet into the air. Scenery covered the forklift so all the audience could see was the boat and the swan and me moving towards the front of the stage. But as we went, somehow a piece of the wooden scenery caught on the forklift and it collapsed with a clatter onto the platform."

Paul's recollection of his reaction to the brouhaha matches Herzog's. "It was happening behind me and I wasn't in any danger, so I just kept singing." The chaos unraveling before the startled audience, and the star tenor's composure, evoked in director Herzog one overwhelming response: "I knew immediately that this was the right guy for my Lohengrin. I thought to myself, 'There is something solid about this man. He's a thoroughly no-nonsense guy. I can get along fine with this guy. He's no prima donna!'"

It was not until curtain calls ended, when Paul attempted to make his way to his dressing room through throngs of press and well-wishers, that he was informed by management that Werner Herzog would like to talk to him in the theater canteen. Paul states his reaction to the message. "I really didn't know who Herzog was; I wasn't a real film watcher, especially of German films."

The messenger quickly filled in Paul to Herzog's importance. "He's important! He's been hired by Wagner to do the new *Lohengrin* for Bayreuth . . ." The deliverer of news raced on: "and they say you're being considered to play the lead role!" Paul recalls his own incredulity at the news. "I laughed when I heard this. 'Bayreuth doesn't consider opera singers from middle houses like Basel,' I told him."

And so, taking the import of the message with a grain of salt, Paul proceeded to meet his visitor in the theater canteen. Herzog and his star tenor's memories converge on the conversation that took place. Herzog remembers: "I told him: 'You're the one I want; you're the Lohengrin I'm looking for. And I hear you used to drive pigs to market. I like you already!'"

Herzog's next words warmed Paul Frey's heart. "He said to me: 'I don't know much about opera, but what you did on stage tonight was obviously very special.'" Still, the invitation to Bayreuth came with a slight reservation. "Herzog was sure he wanted me, but he advised that the big boss of Bayreuth, Wolfgang Wagner, would have the last say. He'd want to see me himself before I got the part for sure."

Such was the importance of getting the right Lohengrin that, over the coming weeks, Wagner sent Henning von Gierke, the head stage director, who'd be designing the stage and costumes for *Lohengrin* at Bayreuth, as well as his orchestra conductor, Peter Schneider, to take a look. "They liked me too but the real test would be Wagner," Paul advises. "If what he saw was good, I'd be in. If not, I'd not stand a chance."

The vignette "Wolfgang Wagner finally meets Paul Frey" would happen quite unexpectedly, and thanks to one of opera's most adored leading men.

46

Mannheim

PAUL WAS NOW SHUTTLING between his home in Basel and Karlsruhe. "I'd taken over the Lohengrin role for the long run, and never saw Klaus König again." He was also finishing the commitment to his Basel contract. Energy percolating, he'd still take on the occasional last-minute replacement role too. "I was a workaholic," he freely admits. Still, there was method in his heavy workload commitment. "I was forty-four years of age. I knew I didn't have an unlimited amount of time to make my mark. The more replacements I took on, the more people who heard me sing, would only benefit my career."

Given the temperamental voices (and personalities) of opera stars, cancellations occurred regularly and last-minute replacements were needed. No doubt, casting directors kept a list of these invaluable performers. And so when a call came to Paul's home one Sunday morning in early 1986, with a fill-in for star tenor Peter Hofmann at the Mannheim gala production of *Lohengrin*, Paul agreed.

He admits that he did so with some reservation. "'Filling in for Peter Hofmann? What a thankless task that will be,' I thought." Few in the European opera world of the late 1970's to mid-1980's hadn't fallen under the powerful spell of the divine Herr Hofmann.

Born in 1944 in Marienbad, Czechoslovakia, Peter Hofmann seemed destined for stardom. Blonde, handsome, with a ringing and clear voice, his early ambition was to be a rock singer.

Mannheim

Hofmann's talents as an operatic singer were still to be discovered. After studying voice at the Karlsruhe Conservatory, he made his operatic debut in 1972 at age twenty-eight in Mozart's The Magic Flute. *Hofmann's blue eyes, blonde hair, and handsome facial features made him the quintessential leading man. His operatic voice, heldentenor, with the characteristic "ping," destined him to sing Wagner.*

The pinnacle of Hofmann's career as a Wagnerian tenor saw him starring in the role of Siegmund in Die Walküre *as part of the Bayreuther Festspiele's 1976 centenary production of Wagner's epic operatic series* Der Ring des Niebelungen. *Critics outdid themselves, praising Hofmann's voice as "ardently lyrical with a heroic edge, but wonderfully expressive, embodying the Nordic spirit."*

But it was Peter Hofmann's physical attributes that set audiences—especially female hearts—aflutter. Bare-chested, tanned, and dressed in tight trousers, Hofmann exuded a sexuality that had never before been witnessed in Bayreuth, nor in any opera house elsewhere. Critics named him a "superstar," one who changed the face of opera.

Hofmann followed his groundbreaking Bayreuth performance with equally lauded ones in Wagner's Parsifal *in 1976 and 1978 and* Lohengrin *in 1979. Now in demand in opera houses around the world, Hofmann radiated celebrity wherever he appeared: at Covent Garden in London, the Met in New York, and the San Francisco Opera. Return appearances at the Holy Grail of Richard Wagner, Bayreuth, were a given.*[63]

Thankless or not, Paul took on the Mannheim job. The decision would turn out to be a providential one. As had occurred more than once in his career, being in the right place at the right time was golden. While stopping short of calling Mannheim an "act of divine providence," Paul does admit: "Somehow it was meant to be that I got the call and that I could go."

He'd been instructed by Mannheim administration to take the train from Basel to Freiburg, Germany. Then he'd be joined on the rest of the journey to Mannheim by the opera house's head stage director. During this "debriefing," the official would prepare the trusty replacement for his assignment that evening.

Paul arrived at the theater with an hour to spare, and immediately moved into wardrobe and makeup. Just as the curtain rose, an opera official stepped on stage to make an announcement.

Part 10: Richard Wagner and Beyond

"Die Rolle des Lohengrin wird heute Abend von Paul Frey gespielt."
"The role of Lohengrin will be played this evening by Paul Frey."

In his dressing room waiting for his call, Paul was unable to hear the message clearly but he knew what had caused the audience's groan. "They were not at all pleased," he laughs. "Coming to see and hear the great Peter Hofmann, and getting instead 'no-name Paul Frey.'"

Paul had another reason to feel pressure on that starry night. He'd been told that Wolfgang Wagner, director of the *Bayreuther Festspielhaus*, was in the audience. Wagner had taken his seat unaware that Peter Hofmann would not play the Lohengrin role. Instead, the tenor of whom he'd heard so much from Werner Herzog, stage designer von Gierke, and orchestra conductor Schneider would be starring. Surely serendipity was playing its anointed part on that most special of evenings.

As for Paul, the Wagner factor added an extra layer of complexity to his performance. "I was aware the whole time that I was on stage that if he didn't like what he saw, he wouldn't offer me a contract, no matter what the others had told him about me." It was with these ominous thoughts that he took the stage that night.

Any disappointment that the audience had felt in the absence of Peter Hofmann vanished from the opening notes of Lohengrin's arrival by swan boat. By the time the curtain went down, it was apparent that a new star had stepped up to rival Wagnerian tenors—including the adored Herr Hofmann.

Warm applause greeted the cast as they took their final bows together. A roar went up from the capacity crowd when Paul Frey had his moment, alone, in the spotlight. Overwhelmed yet gracious, his thoughts centered on one member of the audience.

"I wondered how Wagner was reacting. I knew where he was seated and I had decided to look at him to see his expression. But it took me several curtain calls to summon up enough courage to look him in the eye." And at the very moment that Paul Frey's brown eyes found his... "He was looking right at me—and smiling." Paul gave a Wagnerian-sized sigh of relief. Surely he'd have an opportunity to chat Bayreuth *Lohengrin* with him after the show.

But first, there was the matter of curtain calls. How many of them there were, on that luminous evening, Paul has lost memory. "As long as there's even one audience member standing and cheering, you need to come out for your bows." Convention held too that he should make an attempt to gather up the delivery-truck-load of flowers missiled onto the stage. "I caught some of them like a goalie catches pucks," he jokes. "I guess my hockey years helped with that!"

Informed where Wolfgang Wagner would be waiting to speak to him, Paul hurried to his dressing room to remove costume and make up. But there was one hurdle to jump outside his dressing room before the prize.

"You know, it was unbelievable . . . When I came out of my dressing room . . . the corridors were packed with people. As I started down the steps, cameras started flashing. I was there for half an hour signing autographs. I must have signed my name 100 times before I got away to go to the restaurant. And when I got there the whole restaurant burst into applause." It was a moment of which most performers can only dream . . .

Eventually, with heart thudding, Paul made his way to Wagner's table. Ever the understated Canadian, and despite Wagner's visual reassurance, Paul remained cautious. "I needed to hear the words, 'We want you for Bayreuth' from Wagner's lips." Paul recalls the conversation that would make him an opera star. "I heard that Wagner could be fearsome, but he was very polite, very nice, very ordinary with me."

Paul ventured to confide in Wagner his worries about boldly meeting his gaze during curtain call. "Wagner laughed. 'No, no, we want you!' And I knew I'd be singing at Bayreuth. It was a dream come true." To make the honey even sweeter, Wagner was offering the role to his new Lohengrin without the obligatory audition in Bayreuth. Paul states: "I think I'm one of only a very few who have had this honor."

Media reviews of the Mannheim performance only verified what the audience had seen and expressed. Kristin Marie Guiguet of *Music Magazine* gushed: "Paul Frey's Mannheim performance has instantly placed him among the world's great Wagnerians."[64] Guiguet noted too that from that magical Mannheim evening, the "Paul Frey effect" was immediately felt in other cities where he was scheduled to perform. Tickets for his Basel appearance in von Weber's *Der Freischütz*, which had been 60 percent sold before the Mannheim *Lohengrin*, now were gone in a day. "Suddenly every crowned head of European opera was buying a ticket for this performance, especially to hear Paul Frey sing."[65]

Music writer Pauline Durichen of the *Kitchener-Waterloo Record* also weighed in on "local boy becomes a star." "Suddenly opera directors all over Europe were noticing the ringing heroic voice, with its unusual upper sweetness."[66]

One could have forgiven Paul Frey for returning to home in Basel with stars in his eyes.

47

Bigger and Bigger

WHEN ASKED, IN RETROSPECT, to pinpoint a moment in time when his career moved toward opera stardom, Paul named *Lohengrin* in Karlsruhe. When fame soared, he dates to Mannheim. From the multiple standing ovations and endless bouquets of flowers, to the crush of fans outside his dressing rooms wanting autographs... add to these sweets the glowing and glorious media reviews. Clearly, Peter Hofmann's stand-in had moved to the A-list of opera tenors.

The Mannheim performance was also pivotal to Paul Frey stylistically. "After Mannheim, I began to think of myself not just as an opera singer, but as a Wagnerian opera singer." The growing number of his Wagnerian performances points to the shift.

Between his first Wagner, *Der Fliegende Hollander* in 1983, and Karlsruhe of 1986, only one additional Wagner opera concert appears on Paul Frey's resume. It is *Tannhäuser*. And for that reputed "voice-killer," he did not sing the lead tenor role. "I could never have sung *Tannhäuser* at that time in my career," Paul admits freely. "Nor was I even thinking of myself as a Wagnerian tenor."

Fast-forward to the twelve months between Karlsruhe and Bayreuth, when Paul added fourteen performances of Wagnerian operas to his resume: *Hollander* five times, *Lohengrin* six times, and *Parsifal* three. It's clear where his direction now lay.

Preparing to jump with both feet into the deep and often dark world of Richard Wagner demanded of Paul Frey much more than delving into the composer's language. For Wagner is a composer who makes enormous demands on his singers in terms of voice, stamina, endurance, and preparation.

In an interview with *Kitchener-Waterloo Record* music writer Pauline Durichen in 1987, Paul talks Richard Wagner. "With Wagner, his characterizations, the feeling for how they should be sung, are built right into the notes—motifs, themes, signatures, cross-references . . . You can't just listen to a *Parsifal* or *Lohengrin* and simply 'pick it up' like Mozart or Rossini. It can take much greater effort to appreciate and learn them, but they last longer because you get something more out of the music every time you sing it."[67]

Another key difference between Wagner and the pack is length of the opera performance. Five hours or even more is the norm. And so Wagnerian singers need considerably more stamina than most. Paul was working on this stamina religiously. He was running up to five kilometers a day, doing pushups and regular weight training. "I knew that I had to be in top shape or I just wouldn't be able to handle the demands of the job," he told Durichen.[68]

In his 1987 interview with *Music Magazine*, he reiterated the importance of physical exercise. "My voice depends on the condition of my body. I can be good or bad, depending on the physical shape I'm in."[69]

Then there's the sound that sets Wagnerian opera apart. Wagnerian singers need to have an operatic voice powerful enough to fly over the 120-piece orchestra that the composer demanded. "An orchestra that big makes a huge sound," advises Paul.

Timbre and voice pitch determine Wagnerian stars too. Most are categorized as heldentenors; indeed this voice type is usually synonymous with Wagner. Described by various opera academics as "a tenor who sings dramatic roles" or "a tenor who sings Wagner," the heldentenor presents a "forceful style of singing, but also an accompanying characterization of nobility, strength, and inspirational power."

In her article, "We Need a Hero! The Evolution of the Heldentenor," writer Carla Maria Verdino-Süllwold names the heldentenor voice as being one of "great weight and sonority, particularly strong in the middle and bottom of the voice, in fact a tenor voice with some of the characteristics of a baritone."[70] However, unlike an operatic baritone, the heldentenor also has the ability to sing high.

Verdino-Süllwold calls the divine "ping" the integral component of the Wagnerian heldentenor's voice—"a vocal blessing that has allowed the best Wagnerians to rise above and beyond the voluminous sound of the massive orchestra." While natural ability figures into this serendipity, "distinguished training is essential to finding and developing 'the ping.'"[71]

And how did Paul Frey describe his own operatic voice? Surprisingly not as a heldentenor; nor as a lyric tenor. "It's between the sweetness of the lyric tenor and the richness of the heldentenor," he explained in a 1986 interview with *Music Magazine*. "I can hit a high C but also have that dramatic quality in my voice. I guess you could call me a lyric heldentenor."[72]

The high C benchmark was a significant one—one that Paul Frey's hero, Jon Vickers, either could not or would not attempt.[73]

Finding his niche more than ten years after his operatic career began, Paul Frey thinks back to the conversation that set the wheels in motion for him to grasp the Wagnerian brass ring.

"When intendent Statkus told me that they'd hired Eduardo Villa to take the bulk of the Italian repertoire and that they felt that my niche was in the German, I was a little taken back. Maybe even hurt. But when I thought more about it, Statkus was right. My voice was intended more for Wagner and Strauss and von Weber—German composers. So that definitely pushed me to judge my own strength and make a decision to go for the German territory."

It was a decision that brought just rewards beyond financial and fame. Artistic fulfillment was one. "So many of the story lines of other operas are frankly silly—lightweight. But Wagner's text is so deep, so meaningful, with so many layers. From the singer's point of view—mine at least—every time I sang Wagner I got more out of it. It became a more meaningful opera."

Richard Wagner as a habit-forming drug? Almost. In an interview with the *Montreal Star*'s Paula Citron, Paul admitted to his Wagner obsession: "Once you know Wagner's music, nothing else can compare with it. You can spend years analyzing the relationship between the text and music and still keep finding new things. There are just so many levels."[74]

The world was unfolding quite nicely for Paul Frey. And there were so many treasures to come.

48

Traveling, Traveling Everywhere

PAUL FREY'S PERFORMANCES IN Karlsruhe and later Mannheim had opened the operatic floodgates. News of an ascendant star travels rapidly in the close-knit and competitive European opera world. The next twenty-six months, between *Lohengrin* in Karlsruhe through to the Bayreuth summer of 1987, would see Paul playing the role of Superman—in addition to Knights of the Holy Grail, lotharios, and pirates. Not on the stage, mind you, but in real life. He recalls these heady days:

"It was just go, go, go during these years. I had come into opera late and it had come with a lot of struggle. So I'd need to make the very most of my time. There was no wasting time because an opera singer's career is not a long one."

Over this short period, he'd perform in thirty-three opera productions, as well as four concerts and oratorios. His schedule would take him to nineteen cities—from Copenhagen, Denmark and Dublin, Ireland in the European north, to Montpellier, France in the south. Of particular satisfaction was reprising the role of Lohengrin in Karlsruhe in early 1987. That's where all the "madness" had begun.

He remained on opera directors' lists of last minute fill-ins too. His Peter Hofmann replacement job had brought nothing but bounty, so he was open to others. "If I was available, and the job was something that I liked, I'd have no problem taking it," was his attitude. So when one frantic call came from the Vienna Opera House to prop up ailing megastar Placido Domingo, and he had nothing more on his schedule than watching soccer on TV, he was glad to oblige. But this gig was a little different than usual.

Traveling, Traveling Everywhere

"Domingo wasn't sure if he could get through the whole performance or not. So I was to be there in case he couldn't. Well, how could I turn that down? I hadn't met Domingo yet and this was an opportunity. So I got myself to Vienna, reported that I was there, and as Domingo was planning to at least start Act 1, I'd sit in the audience. During the first intermission, I checked in and he said he was weak; I should get into costume and makeup and wait to take over at a moment's notice in case he couldn't get through Act 2."

And so Paul repaired to a dressing room where costume and makeup folk got him ready. Still the plucky Domingo felt he could begin Act 3 with the assurance that if he passed out on stage, the capable Paul Frey could take over in a moment's notice. Paul finishes the tale of Placido Domingo and his star stand-in.

"And so he finished the entire opera. I got paid for hearing him sing. We had a lovely chat afterwards and he said to me: 'Paul, let me take you out for dinner to thank you for this.' I agreed that would be lovely and I left for home."

Paul calls it a replacement gig like no other.

A rare North American invitation saw Paul appearing in Carl Maria von Weber's *Oberon*, or *The Elf King's Oath*, at the Tanglewood Summer Festival near Boston, Massachusetts. Tanglewood, a woodsy outdoor facility, was the summer home of the Boston Pops Orchestra. It gave Paul an opportunity to compare North American opera audiences—ones he calls "polite but reserved"—with European over-the-top exuberance.

And from Canada? Few engagements came his way. His disappointment about the lack of opportunities from his home country has mellowed over the years, but they remain tangible thirty years later. At the time they were less guarded. In a 1987 interview with Arthur Kaptainis of the *Montreal Gazette*, he is perplexed by the lack of interest from his Canadian performance *alma mater*, the Canadian Opera Company (COC).[75]

"Every time I went back [to Toronto] I would make a point of getting in touch. [COC director] Lofti Mansouri would say, 'Well, I have to hear you.' But in order to hear me he would have to come somewhere where I was singing, and that he never did." Insisting to Kaptainis that he is not bitter—"things are going too well for me to be bitter"[76]—it's clear that hurt lies close to the surface.

Part 10: Richard Wagner and Beyond

Leaving the door open for Canada to call, he insisted to Kaptainis that if and when that invitation came, he wanted it to be on the basis of merit, not nationality. "Do the Canadian opera companies and symphonies owe me something just because I am Canadian? I don't know if they do. I expect them to hire me because I am a good singer."

He'd have some time to wait.

Over this mad, mad, mad period of operatic success, Paul was able to add new repertoire to his resume. And when he did, his first stop was at coach Rainer Altorfer's grand piano. Wagner's *Parsifal* and *Die Meistersinger* and Britten's *Peter Grimes* were now part of his bulging list of operas performed. And while most work came easily, due to his strong memory skills and farm-boy work ethic, not every lesson went smoothly. Paul names *Die Meistersinger* "a very complex piece." "The text and the music repeat themselves, but not identically. And if you sing the wrong words, you'll end up singing the wrong notes. It took me hours and hours to learn it."

Occasionally, there'd be a few days of down time, when he could head home to Basel. Ben, his son, who was four at the time of his parents' relocation, was now a teenager. Paul wished he had more time to spend with the boy. But he always returned home exhausted of body and mind. "So I just collapsed."

Still, this star never second-guessed himself. "I'd waited a long time for success and it hadn't been easy achieving it—especially in the early days. And I knew it wasn't going to last forever." He knew full well that the lifespan for an operatic tenor was short. "So I knew that career had to be put first; it *had* to be put before other things—even time with my family."

Part 11

Lohengrin in Bayreuth

(1987)

49

Being Lohengrin

IN THE MONTHS LEADING up to his Bayreuth appearance in the summer of 1987, Paul Frey had little time to indulge in thoughts of the fame that was surely around his corner. Still, as spring became the summer, he tingled with anticipation of a life-changing experience that, through a rare combination of talent, hard work, and serendipity would be his. He'd be starring in one of Wagner's most-loved operas, in the theater that the composer had envisioned, designed, and built with love.

He recalled his first visit in 1980 to Richard Wagner's "holy grail." His friend Juergen Stutzer, a member of the Basel Stadttheatre chorus when Paul had been with that theater, was now singing in the Bayreuth chorus. Stutzer had secured tickets to the *Festspiele* dress rehearsals for *Parsifal, Der Fliegende Hollander*, and *Lohengrin*. He gave the tickets to Paul, who gladly accepted.

It was the absence of light in the theater that first mesmerized him. "Wagner's theater is unique in that when the lights go down it is completely dark, the orchestra pit being covered. That, in itself, sets the stage for what is to come. Then, when that big sound comes up from seemingly nowhere, it's an overwhelming experience."

Paul enjoyed *Hollander*, having sung it himself on several occasions. The next night was *Parsifal* and Paul fell in love with the story and the production. "When the music came out of that orchestra pit, in the total darkness, it sent shivers up and down my spine."

Night three was *Lohengrin*. "Maybe it was because I didn't have a good seat, but I was less than impressed with the production." "But," he adds,

Part 11: Lohengrin in Bayreuth

"of course, then, I never expected Bayreuth to be a place for me; I never expected to become known as Lohengrin."

Lohengrin *was first staged in Weimar, Germany on August 28, 1850. However, the composer, Richard Wagner, was not conducting, nor was he even in Germany at the time. Wagner had been exiled for his part in the Dresden Uprising the year before. In Weimar, Wagner's close friend, composer Franz Liszt, held the baton. History calls the debut a success. (Wagner was not able to conduct the entire opera himself until 1861 when it was staged in Vienna.)*

Called a romantic opera in three acts, Lohengrin *has, over the decades, proved to be one of Wagner's most accessible and beloved works. The setting is 900 A.D. in the mythical kingdom of Brabant, on the banks of Germany's Schelt River. Disorder and deceit have torn Brabant. Elsa, of royal blood, is accused by the evil Count Telramund and his wife, Ortrud, of having murdered her own brother, Gottfried, who was heir to the throne. Elsa is also said to have invoked a spell that has turned Gottfried into a swan. In truth, it is Ortrud, a witch, who has wielded the magic.*

Elsa, called by the king to defend herself of these charges, dreams of a knight who will save her. Elsa's prayers are answered and a savior magically appears in a boat drawn by a swan. He is Lohengrin, son of Parsifal, and is a Knight of the Holy Grail.

He tells Elsa that he will marry and defend her on one condition: that she cannot ask his name or from where he comes. Lohengrin defeats Telramund and is declared the protector of Brabant.

Telramund and Ortrud swear vengeance. Feigning friendship with Elsa, Ortrud attempts to plant distrust about Lohengrin in her mind. With the support of four noblemen, Telramund accuses Lohengrin of sorcery.

The marriage of Lohengrin and Elsa takes place, although Elsa is troubled by Telramund and Ortrud's evil words. Her doubt causes her to ask the forbidden question: the knight's name. Before Lohengrin replies, Telramund and his supporters burst in on the newly married couple. Lohengrin kills Telramund.

The knight tells Elsa that because she has asked the forbidden question, he must return to the home of his father. The swan returns to pull Lohengrin's boat. It dives into the water, reappearing in the form of Gottfried, Elsa's brother. He will now rule Brabant.

Being Lohengrin

A dove comes down from heaven, and takes the place of the swan at the head of Lohengrin's boat. The knight departs, breaking Elsa's heart. She falls to the ground.

Paul left Basel in early June 1987 to relocate to Bayreuth for the summer. Rehearsals were imminent. He'd rented a house in the town for the duration of the festival. Linda and Ben would join him when they were able.

He shares his thoughts of this pivotal time in his career: "I knew I had to conquer this place or I'd be a flash in the pan. If I wasn't a success, not only would I never be asked back to perform in Bayreuth, but it would damage the forward momentum that my career had been building to since Karlsruhe. Bayreuth was 'it' in Europe, like the Met was in North America."

Regardless of these underlying concerns, it was with a feeling of steely confidence that he approached the bustling Bavarian town of Bayreuth. This tenor was better, stronger, and more seasoned than when Herzog had heard him in Karlsruhe; he was more confident and polished than when Wagner had given his approval in Mannheim. Since then, Paul had appeared in at least forty operatic productions, fourteen of them Wagnerian. Of those, six productions, up to sixty performances, were as the Knight of the Holy Grail. Paul Frey, born in the farming village of Heidelberg, Ontario, was more than ready.

"I was totally confident that I could perform well—more than well—to the very best of my ability. And I knew I had the stamina and the voice." The partnership between voice coach Rainer Altorfer and Paul Frey had prepared, then fine-tuned him to ensure his Bayreuth experience was a glittering success.

50

Working, Working . . .

SETTLING IN TO HIS Bayreuth rental house, Paul was eager to begin *Lohengrin*'s six-week rehearsal period. Werner Herzog's opera would be the star attraction of the 1987 eight-week *Bayreuther Festspiele* or Summer Festival. It would run from the first week in July to late August. One wag called the annual *Festspiele* "the Woodstock of opera."

The director and his head stage and costumer designer, Henning von Gierke, had been in the planning stages for some time. The two had worked previously on several of Herzog's films: *Nosferatu the Vampyre*, *The Enigma of Kaspar Hauser*, and *Fitzcarraldo*. They'd collaborated as well on Herzog's previous foray into opera, *Doktor Faust*, in Bologna.

Given Herzog's reputation as one of the chief inspirations behind the German *avant-garde* film movement (the director's film *Heart of Glass* was produced with the entire cast under hypnosis) and Gierke's credentials as a star in his field—he'd won design awards for *The Enigma House* and *Nosferatu*—much was expected from this partnership. The unexpected, the exalted, and the surreal would surely make *Lohengrin* the marquee performance at the 1987 *Bayreuther Festspiele*.

Rehearsals began in an open studio setting with the principal cast: Paul Frey as Lohengrin, Nadine Secunda as Elsa, Ekkehard Wlaschiha as Telramund, Gabriele Schnaut as Ortrud, and Manfred Schenk as King Heinrich. Herzog, von Gierke, Bayreuth orchestra conductor Peter Schneider, and other essential personnel joined the cast, seated in a roundtable setting. The

Working, Working . . .

large chorus needed for this production—over 100 singers—would begin rehearsals later.

Herzog, the star director, was the key to putting his unique stamp on this *Lohengrin*. "Given Herzog's fame, I wondered what he would be like to work with—maybe difficult; maybe unapproachable," recalls Paul. "But he was none of those things; he was open and approachable—funny too."

A director who, it seems, could ruffle the feathers of the Bayreuth "old guard." In an interview for this book, Herzog recalled the horror with which his request of head Bayreuth conductor Peter Schneider during one rehearsal to "stop the band" was greeted. "All I could hear were screams of delight from the orchestra pit below," he laughed. "I guess they couldn't believe that someone had called them 'a band.'"[77] "Herzog was a man who loved to say outrageous things," Paul Frey offered, with a grin.

Approachable, yes, with a sense of humor, yes, but Herzog was also a seasoned professional who knew exactly what he wanted. He also had the expertise to guide his cast toward his vision. Paul remembers an early rehearsal scene that pitted Lohengrin in a sword fight against the archvillain, Telramund, played by Ekkehard Wlaschiha. Paul was able to wield his weapon to the director's satisfaction; Ekkehard Wlaschiha was not. "He just couldn't get the hang of it, so Herzog picked up the weapon and expertly showed Ekkehard how to do it—no swords touching of course. I was impressed. This guy is a both a movie guy and a stage guy. He knows what he's doing."

Set designer von Gierke had constructed a three-dimensional model of the stage to allow the cast to better interpret his vision. Starkly minimalist was the theme of this version of Wagner's opera. Past productions had seen it set in a royal court, with the cast in Elizabethan dress and bewigged; another saw cast in *lederhosen* and *dirndls*. More eccentric visions saw *Lohengrin* taking place in a dollhouse. Still another played out in a schoolroom, the chorus performing as school children in short pants and middies, throwing paper airplanes at each other. No doubt in an aim to lure a younger audience, another *Lohengrin* was placed in contemporary times, with the chorus in t-shirts and blue jeans.

Von Gierke's *Lohengrin*, set in the mythical northern kingdom of Brabant in the tenth century, evolves in the out-of-doors. It's an unforgiving and harsh land of ice and snow, of rocky outcrops, stunted grasses, and chilling waters. *Globe and Mail* critic Robert Everett-Green summarizes it as "complete with skins, shields and druidic rocks."[78]

Part 11: Lohengrin in Bayreuth

Costumes, also conceptualized and designed by von Gierke, reflected the medieval, northern European setting. Both men and women were draped in heavy, loose, mid- to floor-length garments. Furs enveloped both King Heinrich and Telramund. Virginal Elsa was gowned in soft and flowing white, while the witch Ortrud was resplendent in symbolic scarlet.

Considerable attention and thought took place regarding Lohengrin's costumes. Reflecting Herzog's vision of the hero as a prince of peace, not a warrior, von Gierke initially clothed his barefoot knight in a knee-length, tent-like tunic. Paul took an instant dislike to his garb.

"I looked like the duck that came in with the swan—with my bare feet sticking out of a tent." Not wanting to play the *prima donna* by complaining about his costume, Paul patiently submitted to the concept. Eventually, and to his relief, von Gierke came to his tenor with the confession that Lohengrin's dress required rethinking. "Thank goodness for that," laughs Paul. Instead, he would be variously dressed in floor-length garments in shades of heavenly blue. On his feet: soft boots.

But it was the special effects—dazzling by mid-1980's operatic technology—that would put the "wow" factor in the Herzog/von Gierke production. From Lohengrin's arrival in a swirl of blue light and laser—"like an emissary from the heavens,"[79] extolls Robert Everett-Green—to the rolling waves on the stage; to Prince Gottfried conjured from a dead swan at the opera's denouement, von Gierke and Herzog combined their considerable skills, using cutting-edge technology to offer sheer magic to Bayreuth's adoring audiences.

Opening night saw Paul Frey in his dressing room, costumed and made up for his role. He welcomed *Bayreuther Festspiele* director Wolfgang Wagner, who had dropped by to wish him luck. The two exchanged pleasantries before Wagner commented on the unfortunate illness of Nadine Secunda, Herzog's Elsa. In the same breath, he noted her replacement, Catarina Ligendza. Paul recalls the conversation:

"I was stunned by Wagner's news and showed it on my face. 'It's obvious from your reaction that you didn't know this,' he told me." Paul indicated that this was indeed the case. "So with five minutes to the curtain going up, I found out that the soprano who I'd been rehearsing with for the past six weeks, the singer I'd appeared with several times before, who I knew well, was *not* singing tonight. And she was being replaced with someone

Working, Working . . .

I'd never sung with before." The professional who'd once been given the thankless job of replacing god Peter Hofmann and had turned dust into gold weathered Wagner's news with his customary aplomb. "And it turned out fine," recalls Paul.

Paul reflects on his feelings as he stepped out of his swan boat and sang for the first time at Bayreuth. "Even though I felt I was ready for the role and could do it justice, I had carried a fair amount of stress since I'd signed the contract." This trepidation carried throughout opening night evening. "You just never know how things stand until the audience reacts."

And react they did, with unbridled enthusiasm. Curtain call after curtain call only reinforced Paul's self-confidence that, at least for the *Bayreuther Festspiele* season of 1987, *Lohengrin* was indeed his.

Paul stood for his final bow with a monumental load lifted off his shoulders. The next test would come from the critics' reviews. Calling him a "clarion-voiced Lohengrin, quite formidable," critic Donal Henahan of the *New York Times* predicted that "if his [Frey's] bright, firmly-focused tenor does not give out from strain at a tender age, as regularly happens with promising Wagnerians, Mr. Frey is likely to become one of the world's most employable heldentenors."[80]

The *Globe and Mail*'s music critic Robert Everett-Green lauded that "Frey's performance was everything that should be expected from the most important Canadian tenor to emerge since Jon Vickers."[81] *London Free Press* journalist Ed Krawchyk called Paul Frey "a nearly perfect Lohengrin, vocally and visually."[82] Krawchyk also reported that "one ardent Wagnerian described Frey as 'the reincarnation of the great Ramon Vinay.'"

Bayreuth Festival's press officer also recounted for Krawchyk that "two cabs were needed to deliver bouquets of flowers to be tossed toward the singer during his solo curtain call." In response, Paul joked: "I caught each one as it was tossed on the fly. Again my hockey training had something to do with it."[83]

51

Dealing with Fame

BEFORE BAYREUTH, IF ASKED to name his most rabid, most enthusiastic of audiences, Paul Frey would have responded: "Karlsruhe." He now gave Bayreuth crowds equal footing on the enthusiasm scale. Flowers, gifts, and requests for autographs became standard.

Unique among other operatic venues, Bayreuth offered a designated time period each week during *Festspiele* season where the general public could queue at a location in the town for autographs. The line-up for a Paul Frey autograph usually stretched a block. Visitors came from around the world, including Canada, the U.S., and South America. Some had waited a number of years for the chance to buy tickets.

A measure of the success of any long-run performance is the number of celebrities it attracts. In Germany of 1987, there was no bigger star than Chancellor Helmut Kohl. So when news reached the *Lohengrin* cast that Kohl was in the audience, most, including Lohengrin himself, looked forward to meeting the politician at a post-performance reception. Paul recalls:

"He knew that I was Canadian and asked me where I was born and raised. I told him in Heidelberg, which was a village outside Kitchener, Ontario. I never expected he'd have ever heard of the city, but he surprised me: 'Kitchener... that used to be called Berlin, didn't it? Mulroney told me that' [a reference to then Canadian Prime Minister Brian Mulroney]."

Star-studded receptions were the norm for the *Bayreuther Festspiele*, with Paul Frey routinely the center of attention. Yet, there was a down side to sitting on top of the opera world. "Mellowing after a performance was the trick," admits Paul Frey. "Often there'd be receptions and social events after the show. Lots of noise; lots of alcohol and food. Eventually you'd get

Dealing with Fame

back to your bed but turning off the noise in your head was tough. Sometimes you didn't get to sleep until 5 a.m." Uppers and downers didn't often infiltrate the opera world in the heady 1980's and 1990's like they did the rock music scene, but alcohol and sleeping pills were often *de rigeur* for survival.

Outside one or two performances a week and the autograph sessions, Paul and the other cast members of *Lohengrin* had time to spare. Set in an agricultural area of Germany, Bayreuth and the surrounding area offered long country drives and idyllic scenery. "It was lovely for a country boy like me," says Paul. And so a leisurely drive exploring the area was tonic for relaxation. The occasional golf game with colleagues and dining in various local restaurants also filled the hours. And always there was the requisite exercise—five kilometers a day, up and down the hills around Bayreuth. Stamina was essential for enduring a five-hour Wagnerian opera. "My voice depends on my body being in top shape," Paul regularly told interviewers.

A town whose identity, especially in *Festspiele* season, was linked to the opera house, Bayreuth had become used to opera stars in their midst. And for the most part, they were given space outside the *Haus*. "I never got mobbed like movie stars and rock singers do when they're out and about," says Paul. "Maybe a polite request for an autograph at a restaurant, but not too much more than that."

That's not to say that being a Bayreuth star didn't have its perks. Driving from his rented house to the theater usually saw Paul parking in a metered spot. And more often than not, when he returned, he'd find a parking ticket. "I had a whole glove box of them and intended, at some point, to go to the parking authority and pay my bill," he confesses. One day, heading to his car after a rehearsal, he found an officer of the law in the very midst of putting a parking ticket under his windshield wiper. Paul recounts the scenario:

"I walked up to him, apologized for the infraction, and said that I'd take care of them. The policeman looked at me and said: 'You're Lohengrin, aren't you?' I said I was. He smiled and shook my hand. Then he took off his hat, which was white on the top, saying: 'If you'll give me your autograph on my hat, I'll forget about this ticket and all the ones before.' I protested but he insisted. And I never got another parking ticket."

Grateful at the time that he didn't have to pay his fine, given more thought, the incident caused Paul to question his celebrity status. "People are always telling you how much they like you, admire you; they want to talk to you, they want to touch you. So you need to work hard to keep your ego in check. And if you don't, there's a real possibility that you'll get to believe all these complimentary things that people are telling you all the time." He then warns: "And when that happens, you get to the point that you believe what you hear—that you are special. And you begin to expect things that you never did when you weren't 'special.'"

Celebrity was fine for Paul Frey in the short term. "But living like this for the long run? Not for me." On the top of the world, Paul remained, in essence, a product of his Mennonite heritage.

Part 12

After Lohengrin:
On Top of the Opera World

(1987–1990)

52

No Rest for This Tenor

WERNER HERZOG'S GLITTERING JEWEL wrapped the 1987 *Bayreuther Festspiele* season with as much fanfare as it had opened it. Those opera lovers who hadn't been able to secure tickets could wait for the 1988 season. Paul had already committed to return.[84]

The fondness that Paul felt for Bayreuth was clear in an interview with the *London Free Press* on August 22, 1987. He admitted: "I would have sung there for free . . . The atmosphere is unbelievably exciting and you get to learn so much from so many great singers."[85]

His love affair with Bayreuth was in direct contrast to Jon Vickers'. In her unauthorized biography of Vickers, *John Vickers: A Hero's Life*, writer Jeannie Williams stated that the Canadian tenor "hated Bayreuth" and categorized the annual *Festspiele* as a "Black Mass." "All those people walking up the hill to the shrine—homosexuals, men with other men's wives . . . I hated it. I was revolted by it."[86]

Sometime over that glorious Bayreuth summer, Paul Frey had also come to the decision that his future lay in Europe, not Canada. He'd arrived, green, in Basel ten years before, with the idea that his would be a five-year stint. Five years had grown into ten years and now the cards seemed to indicate a longer residency.

The Freys had become Swiss citizens in 1984 and Paul admits that they'd made the move more for their son, Ben, than themselves. "Ben was four when we'd arrived, but he was growing up as a Swiss, not a Canadian." Paul and Linda felt it was best for their son to be a dual Swiss-Canadian citizen as he approached his teenage years. Ironically, Ben Frey wasn't pleased about the choice. At age eighteen, Swiss males needed to do six weeks of compulsory military service. "And Ben didn't like this at all," Paul remembers.

Post-Bayreuth, Paul was also making other modifications to his professional life. He told music critic Robert Everett-Green of the *Globe and Mail*: "Up until now, I've always let other people tell me what I should do next, because of my background (a reference to his Mennonite, pacifist roots). But no more."[87] Clearly, a more authoritative, confident Paul Frey was on the horizon.

Despite lobbying from critics and opera insiders, one role he'd decided to stay away from was Siegfried in Wagner's opera *Siegfried*. "Far too long and very hard on the voice," he explains. And what roles was he looking forward to? The role of Siegmund in *Die Walküre*, for one. "Wonderful to sing," he volunteers, "and not quite so long."[88]

He'd committed himself to burn the midnight oil to achieve his goals. In a 1987 interview with the *Kitchener-Waterloo Record*, he vowed: "For the next couple of years, my life has to be 150%, there's no getting around it."[89]

53

To the Top: The Met

RETURNING HOME TO BASEL for a few days of relaxation and family visiting before he was due to hop on the Frey musical merry-go-round again, Paul answered his door to reveal an (initially) unwelcome visitor. "Standing there was Alan Green, the agent from Columbia Artists Management who had brushed me off a few years before," states Paul. "My first inclination was to slam the door in his face."

We'll eavesdrop on the awkward doorway conversation that followed.

Alan Green: "Might I have a few minutes of your time, Paul?"

Paul (gruffly): "Well, you didn't have much time for me the last time we met. I remember you were pretty quick to usher me out your door in New York."

Raised with Canadian country politeness, Paul still allows the agent to step in.

Alan Green: "Are you still interested in Columbia representing you?"

Paul stifles a derisive laugh, but the visitor, expecting the singer's response, is ready.

Alan Green: "Just hold on and hear out what I have to say . . ."

Not being shown the door, Green forges on.

Alan Green: "Back when I met you in New York, you were just a house singer in Basel—a second or third-tier European opera house—a dime a dozen. Even though I was very impressed with your voice at the time I heard you, I knew that I'd have little luck representing you in most of the larger venues. Basel just doesn't have much prestige.

Paul: "I'm listening."

Part 12: After Lohengrin: On Top of the Opera World

Alan Green: "But now, you've sung to great acclaim in Bayreuth. You're big news and I can sell you anywhere—at the biggest opera houses in the world. Paul Frey is now a SOMEBODY."

"And I fully understood this," Paul admits. "Right then and there I signed a contract with Columbia Artists. And they represented me well in Canada and the U.S. over the years."

A booking at the Metropolitan Opera House in New York City was proof that Alan Green and Columbia Artists Management were worth the commission Paul Frey paid.

September 23, 1987 would see Paul Frey at the Holy Grail of North American opera: the Metropolitan Opera House in New York City. He'd be singing the lead role of Bacchus in Richard Strauss's *Ariadne auf Naxos*. American soprano Jessye Norman would pair with him as Ariadne. The opera had the reputation of being challenging for both tenor and soprano voices. "Some called it a tenor-killing role," reports Paul. It was also a prize.

In an interview with the *Montreal Star*'s Arthur Kaptainis, Paul spoke of the honor of being asked to sing at the Met. "Of course to any North American, the Met is the pinnacle. When the phone rings and you feel like joking, you say: 'It must be the Met.'"[90] No joking now. Paul Frey *had* been asked.

After the thrill of the Met invitation passed, apprehension crept into the soul of Canadian Paul Frey. "Yes, I was very nervous about singing at the Met because of its status. It is, for North American opera, the pinnacle of success." And while Paul rationalized that his emotions were "quite silly, because for my career, singing at the Met was not as important as singing in Bayreuth," the reality was that the place set his heart to pounding.

Costumed, made up, and ready to sing, Paul waited behind the stage curtain for his cue. (The first three lines of the *Ariadne auf Naxos* score are performed offstage). "I looked at the stage director beside me and the monitor above me and my heart was pounding so much I thought it would come through my chest! I was having a panic attack!"

Then the terror passed and Paul gave his customary outstanding performance. Kaptainis quotes Met artistic director James Levine's praise: "It might have been the first time in the company's history that a perfect Ariadne's voice had been matched with a perfect Bacchus' voice."[91]

The Kaptainis interview was also Paul Frey's chance to voice his frustration with the continuing dearth of opportunities for Canadians to sing in their own country. "To hear Canadians in leading parts, we must go south or across the Atlantic," he complained. "To hear Americans or Europeans we need only stay put." Paul Frey's exasperation went beyond attitude to facilities. "Toronto opera goers and performers alike are handicapped by the poor acoustics and lack of technical facilities at the O'Keefe Centre..."[92]

And more disappointment was to come.

54

It Has to Be 150 Percent

PAUL FREY TURNED FORTY-SEVEN on April 20, 1988. He was, by his own reckoning, "in the very prime of my career." And fulfilling his aim to give "150 percent of myself to my career," between January 1988 and December 1989 he accepted thirty-six invitations to sing. They included opera, concert, and oratorio engagements and ranged from one-night bookings to twenty-performance opera runs.

Reprising his role as Lohengrin in the *Bayreuther Festspiele* seasons of 1988 and 1989 only solidified his stature as their reigning Prince. "Wolfgang Wagner felt that I had the perfect voice for Lohengrin. I loved it myself and felt I sang it well, so the situation benefitted us both." It seems that audiences and critics couldn't be happier either.

Toronto *Globe and Mail*'s Robert Everett-Green, a confirmed Frey fan by now, put his stamp of approval on *Lohengrin*'s second season: "It was the kind of performance that impresses immediately by the thought and depth of preparation that has gone into its making—immediately and for a long time afterward, when the vividness of individual moments have faded."[93]

Paul's strong performances in Bayreuth opened the door to invitations from around the opera world. A last-minute call in 1988 from the Royal Opera House at Covent Garden in London added that historic opera building to his "sung there" list. The circumstances had been serendipitous and included some *déjà vu*.

Again, superstar tenor Placido Domingo was ailing—this time seriously—and could Paul Frey stand in for him in *Lohengrin*? "Most definitely," said the amiable tenor. It seems the London crowd didn't miss Domingo that much, giving the Canadian a five-minute standing ovation.

It Has to Be 150 Percent

His performance invited half a dozen appearances at Covent Garden over the next decade.

With a 1988 invitation to sing in East Germany, Paul performed, for the first time, behind the Iron Curtain. Since the 1961 construction of the concrete and barbed wire *Antifascistischer Schutzwall*, or "antifascist bulwark,"[94] between East and West Berlin, appearances by Western performers came with restrictions. Paul Frey was one of the earliest Western artists invited behind the Iron Curtain. He'd be giving a concert in the historic Berlin Concert Hall presenting excerpts from Wagner's operas. One year before the wall fell, Paul gained a personal insight into the politics of Western artists appearing in the East.

"East German police picked me up at 'Checkpoint Charlie', the most often-used crossing point of the wall between East and West Berlin, before the concert. I was driven to the Berlin Concert Hall and as soon as the concert was over, the police were there to pick me up and deliver me back to where they had picked me up in West Berlin." Paul laughs, wondering if the authorities were worried that he was at a risk to flee to the East.[95]

1988 also saw his first visit to Australia to perform the lead role of Walther von Stolzing in Wagner's "comedy" *Die Meistersinger von Nürnberg*. The production, a generous gift from the German government to the people of Australia, saw Paul performing at the Sydney Opera House. Put up in a luxury apartment, along with other cast and crew, he'd remain in the city for six weeks.

"The walk to the opera house each day from the apartment was through the Sydney Botanical Garden," Paul recalls fondly. "What a treat that was! Then, just as you were nearing the end of the garden, the spectacular white opera house built right on the water came into view. It was just stunning." Paul also had a ringside seat for the arrival of an armada of seagoing schooners and a fireworks display during Australia Day celebrations. So far away from his ancestral home, Paul felt an uncharacteristic longing for Canada.

The safety and security of Sydney was in direct contrast to Tel Aviv in the Jewish state of Israel. There Paul and the Cologne Opera Company performed *Fidelio*. With political tensions high, the city was constantly patrolled by armed Israeli soldiers. "Travel was restricted too," says Paul. "Linda was with me on this trip and both of us wanted to travel to Jerusalem but were told it was too dangerous."

Part 12: After Lohengrin: On Top of the Opera World

Paul returned to Italy in 1989. And what a difference eight years could make. Back in 1981, driving a beat-up Audi to Genoa (and returning to his car to find it vandalized), Paul now crossed the border into Italy in much different circumstances. An invitation had come to sing *Oberon* at Milan's La Scala. Considered one of the premier opera houses in the world, La Scala (official name *Teatro alla Scala*), opened in 1778. It proudly carried with its history the prestige of premiering some of Italy's greatest operas: Verdi's *Otello* (1887) and *Falstaff* (1893), and Puccini's *Madama Butterfly* (1904), among others.

Milan in particular, and Italian opera houses in general, were by his own admission not Paul's favorite venues. Still, his comments are more diplomatic than fellow Canadian Jon Vickers'. Vickers called Italian opera personnel "chauvinistic," and the industry "brimming with prima donnas." "Life is too short to have to deal with them," the Canadian virtuoso huffed.[96]

Paul's issues were more performance-based than with the national character. They included a lack of punctuality at La Scala and in other Italian houses. "It didn't seem to matter if they got started at 8 p.m. or 9 p.m. or whenever." Inattention to detail was also a hallmark of Italian opera. "You'd be using a prop in a performance that you'd never had before in rehearsals." To the *London Free Press*' Ed Krawchyk, he vowed: "I wouldn't care if I never went back, so shoddy were the attitudes of the production team."[97]

55

An Invitation with a Difference

A 1989 INVITATION TO sing *Lohengrin* at the San Francisco Opera caught Paul by surprise. And it delighted him! The offer had come from the new San Francisco Opera director, Lofti Mansouri, late of the Canadian Opera Company. Over Paul's years in Basel, he'd felt "shunned" by the COC, the same organization that had stationed him in the chorus during two of his three years at the University of Toronto Opera School (see chapter 48).

Paul had previously done an interview with Arthur Kaptanis of the *Montreal Star* after his first Bayreuth *Lohengrin*. The subject of that story was "Paul Frey and the COC problem." After that revelation, the Canadian press picked up on the situation and, Paul reports, when members of the press inquired of the COC the reason for the exclusion, "Mansouri as spokesperson always stated they'd tried to get me but I was always busy." That, stresses Paul Frey "was simply not true."

When, soon after Mansouri's promotion to the San Francisco Opera Company, Paul got a call from him to sing *Lohengrin*, he gladly accepted. The COC issue was never discussed between singer and administrator. "Mansouri was thrilled to be in San Francisco; he was delighted to have me sing *Lohengrin* and I was glad to be there. Why spoil it with talk of the COC?" Clearly, Paul Frey flew under the "let sleeping dogs lie" banner.

Several days before he was to fly to San Francisco, the city was struck by a magnitude 6.3 earthquake. Sixty-three people were dead, with almost 3,800 injured. Widespread damage to buildings was reported, with hundreds of citizens homeless, and businesses destroyed. Not surprisingly, Paul took a call at home indicting that, in all likelihood, the concert would be

Part 12: After Lohengrin: On Top of the Opera World

cancelled and need to be rescheduled. Two days later, Paul was informed that the opera was to go ahead.

Driving into the city from the airport, Paul was surprised at the level of damage resulting from the earthquake. But in the old part of the city, most of the solid, cement buildings, including the opera house, built in 1932, were largely undamaged. The only repair needed was ceiling cracks, which were now being protected from falling by nets.

Paul had another reason to look forward to San Francisco. He'd been contacted by the producers of the CBC television series *Adrienne Clarkson Presents*. Hosted by the well-respected journalist Adrienne Clarkson,[98] the program wished to devote the entire hour to Paul Frey and his luminous career. His appearance in San Francisco as Lohengrin would be the jumping off point for the episode.

With cameras set to roll and Ms. Clarkson prepped, the unexpected occurred. For the first time in his career, Paul Frey had come down sick. Laryngitis, that plague of singers, no matter their specialty, had struck. He was going to have to cancel at least one of the performances.

Switching gears, *Adrienne Clarkson Presents* producers chose to incorporate this misfortune into the hour's program. Paul is shown fretting at this turn of events as he waits out the storm in his apartment. "This has never happened to me in twelve years of performing," laments the tenor.

Paul Frey's illness allowed viewers a glimpse of the man behind the star: one whose family and cultural background values a stellar work ethic, reliability, and determination. Paul is viewed speculating on his life were he not able to sing—if opera were now denied. It marks a rare glimpse of a performer's inner fears.

Frey's unexpected illness has sent opera house director Mansouri into action. With television cameras running, Mansouri has directed a staff member to get Canadian tenor Ben Heppner on the line and hopefully fill in for Frey until the latter is fit to return. A pre-fame (and nervous) young Heppner is shown arriving in San Francisco. With the score of *Lohengrin* in hand, Heppner[99] frets about whether he can perform the fill-in role to satisfaction. Paul Frey's absence was a short-lived one and he returned in the next *Lohengrin* performance, up to his usual standards and voice.

For the Canadian television audience, Mansouri, clearly a Paul Frey fan, praises his star. "He has the right type of voice to sing Wagner—lyricism

An Invitation with a Difference

and power in voice but doesn't look like a Wagnerian" (a reference to Paul's slim and trim build).

The year also saw Paul back Kitchener-Waterloo for his first performance since 1984. At that time, still contracted to Basel, Paul was warmly welcomed as "local boy done good." Now, the star of the *Bayreuther Festspiele*'s *Lohengrin*, adored performer at Covent Garden, La Scala, the Paris Opera House, and New York's Met, adulation for him knew no bounds.

To the Centre in the Square's sold-out crowd, Paul presented a twenty-song repertoire of classical, operatic, and pop selections. Paul calls it "an amazing night. It was just me and a piano." In a later interview with Scott Tracey of the *Guelph Mercury*, he describes the emotions singing before a hometown crowd. "I'm always happy to return to my home area because I have a lot of friends and family there." But he adds: "it's always frightening performing for [them.]"[100]

Toronto also had an opportunity to applaud this graduate of the Toronto Opera School and a former member of the Canadian Opera Company. He'd been booked for a performance of *Die Walküre* at Roy Thompson Hall. But Canadian audiences wouldn't see Wagner's work in opera form, but in concert. And the company supporting him wouldn't be the COC, but the Toronto Symphony. The situation between Paul Frey, world-class opera tenor, and his home and native land remained a curious one, seven years after he left Canada.

Constantly in demand in Germany—in Munich, Berlin, Cologne, Stuttgart, Mannheim—Paul had his favorite venues in that opera-mad nation. "Karlsruhe was always wonderful and the audiences were so appreciative, but I was always treated very well in Munich and Berlin too." But one invitation to reprise *Lohengrin* at the Stuttgart Opera House in late 1989 left him with a decidedly cool feeling.

Paul explains that with oft-performed operas, like plays, stage directors are always looking for novelty—exotic settings, unique costumes, obscure time periods. The genial Canadian was usually fine with whatever twist the powers that be came up with for a reprise of a popular opera—except one.

"The Stuttgart idea was that Lohengrin comes from outer space. He enters the stage from above, wearing a space suit and a helmet. Then he

Part 12: After Lohengrin: On Top of the Opera World

walks down a slope to the stage." While the space theme itself was, he felt, pushing innovation to the extreme, he would do it. However, he would not, as plans called for, walk down the ramp wearing a helmet. "It was unsafe and I refused."

A compromise was made in that Lohengrin, in his extra-terrestrial suit, would walk down the slope *carrying* his space helmet. Still, the difference of opinion marked him as "difficult." "And I was never called to sing in Stuttgart again." "Remember," Paul advises, "singers are a dime a dozen and can be easily replaced. Stage directors, on the other hand are few."

But with a new decade before him, Paul Frey could only see stars ahead. "Things were good. I was working like a madman, but it was great." Ahead, the 1990's would surely bring new achievements, accolades, and challenges. They would also bring his first major career disappointment.

Part 13

A Career Disappointment and a Well-Deserved Honor

(1990–2005)

56

Strike Out for Canada

AS A NEW DECADE opened, Paul Frey forged ahead—"150 percent" by his own estimation. In addition to his numerous opera bookings, he gladly took concert and oratorio gigs.[101] Paul enjoyed both. "Doing opera, you can take refuge behind your makeup and costume. But in a recital you're totally exposed, with only your accompanist and the grand piano to lean on."

Beethoven's *Ninth Symphony* topped the list of his most requested concerts, with nineteen over these years. Six of those invitations came from Canada. Handel's *Messiah* was Paul's most requested oratorio, with all nine bookings Canadian. These gigs surely persuaded him that the dearth of invitations from home had more to do with opera's low profile in Canada, hence financial, than any issue with the performer.

So he'd been heartened when in January 1990, three years after his breakthrough in Bayreuth, there seemed to be stirring from the Canadian opera establishment. He'd received an invitation to sing *Lohengrin* with the Canadian Opera Company in Toronto. Finally! The opera would be staged at Toronto's O'Keefe Centre for seven performances in 1993. Paul was delighted. It had taken fifteen years, but Canada was finally recognizing his outstanding achievements.

It seems that Paul hadn't been alone in noticing the slight. In September of 1987, a month after his first Bayreuth appearance, William Littler of the *Toronto Star* in his article "Tenor wins international fame for Canada,"[102] noted: "Canada didn't pay much attention to Paul Frey in the couple of years following his operatic studies in Toronto, and Europe has since become his home." Littler had gone on to say that "we too need the services of an international class heldentenor from time to time . . ." Littler

Part 13: A Career Disappointment and a Well-Deserved Honor

was leading a Paul Frey cheering section lobbying for a *"gastspiel"* (guest performance) to "lure him back."

Don't rush things in the world of Canadian opera though! Four years after Littler's entreaty, the COC's invitation had finally come in the mail.

Paul had little time to consider Canada as he plunged into a new decade of his bright and shiny professional life. Looking back on the blur of these years he calls himself "a workaholic." There was both personal and financial reason for his strong ethic. "My success really hadn't come until I was in my late forties. I figured that I had ten to fifteen years until my voice couldn't carry me to the same level, and I'd have to step back. So I wanted to make the very best use of the time I had in front of me."

With no pension, healthcare, or benefits, it was in his best interests to work as much as he could, and put money away for the proverbial "rainy day." No doubt, images of Wagnerian god Peter Hofmann swam before him in this respect. After Hofmann's opera career had faded, he had made his living in musical theater and had a successful run as the elusive Phantom in Andrew Lloyd Webber's *Phantom of the Opera*. But by then, Hofmann was struggling with Parkinson's disease and dementia. The darling of Bayreuth lived his final years in poverty, cared for by an ex-wife until his death in November 2010.

Paul had no intention of following in these financial footsteps. "In the early 1990's, I was doing very well financially, but I worked constantly and took no holidays. My life was travel, perform, travel, perform . . ."

The new decade also brought *Lohengrin* to film. During the 1991 *Bayreuther Festspiele* season, film crews set up and Werner Herzog returned to oversee the production. Paul Frey reprised his role as Lohengrin, Gabriele Schnaut returned as Ortrud, Ekkehard Wlaschira as Telramund, and Manfred Schenk as King Heinrich. American Cheryl Studer replaced Natalia Secunda as Elsa.

The opera would be filmed and recorded over six separate segments. No audience would be present. As was the case with all film work, if the director was not satisfied with a particular take, it would be repeated. Paul calls the *Lohengrin* filming "grueling." "Some scenes had to be done many times to get what Herzog wanted." As movie work took place in addition to the regular live performances, the extra load was difficult for the cast. "We were all relieved when it was over," says Paul.

Bookings in parts of the world not yet explored defined Paul Frey's decade. A favorite was Buenos Aires, Argentina. With a five-tier horseshoe-shaped opera house as large and as grand as the Met, and wildly enthusiastic fans, this South American venue was a treasure. It came with some history too. Paul had become friendly with the theater's German conductor and commented to him on the always-electric mood.

"He told me that many of the city's operagoers were former Nazis who'd fled Germany at the end of the war. The other large group of opera lovers were German Jews who'd escaped the Nazis, either before or during World War II." The irony was, the conductor related, that forty years later the two groups had no idea of each other's pasts. "They could have been sitting side by side in the theater—simply united in their love of German opera."

An invitation to sing Mahler's *Eighth Symphony* in Tokyo introduced him to the Japanese operagoer. "They were enthusiastic but much less boisterous than the South Americans." He calls from his memory a polite knock on his dressing room door and opening it to find a teenage Japanese fan.

"She had a DVD of *Lohengrin* with her and in her broken English told me she just loved it—it was her favorite opera." The girl then presented the disc, shyly asking her hero to sign it. "She was thrilled and before she left she gave me a lovely pair of socks!" Paul accepted the unusual offering graciously and notes that, decades later, he still wears the fan's thoughtful gift.

57

A Dark Cloud over the Met

As 1991 opened, Paul Frey was surely on top of the world. Bookings poured in, his performances were glowingly reviewed, and his financial "nest egg" for retirement was growing. Then a call from Toronto rained on his parade.

One year after the booking to sing *Lohengrin* in Toronto, the Canadian Opera Company cancelled. "High cost was the explanation," he recalls of the communication. Not given to outbursts of anger, Paul was still furious. And he struck back. "It was a legal contract and I had turned down other invitations to take the COC booking. I insisted they pay the full amount. And they did."

A 1991 appearance in Madrid singing Strauss's *Ariadne auf Naxos* had brought another dark cloud. "When I took my solo bow at the end of the performance, along with the applause, I heard a few boos. It shocked me. I'd never been booed before." Paul's concern was heightened as he'd been praised during warm-up by the ever-upbeat Rudolph Bautz, his coach.

"So I listened to a recording of the performance and, yes, my voice sounded quite raw in spots. It wasn't the same voice that had first sung *Lohengrin* at Bayreuth." And while he could convince himself that the discordance was the effect of illness or fatigue, and he was not yet ready to bid a fond farewell to the opera life, there was a more serious problem at hand: Rudolph Bautz. "Rudolph said everything was wonderful before the Madrid concert. But Rudolph always said *everything* was wonderful. I felt I couldn't trust his judgment any longer." And so, Paul Frey and Rudolph Bautz parted ways. "I felt bad. I liked him very much, but I had to do this."

A Dark Cloud over the Met

1991. Not a banner year on Paul Frey's personal calendar. And still the early 1990's weren't done with him yet. *Les Troyens*, with a reputation as an operatic monster, was planning on taking a bite in 1993.

A second invitation from the Metropolitan in New York City shone ahead like a beacon for Paul Frey. He was booked to perform *Les Troyens* (*The Trojans*), starring as Aeneas. A coup, for sure, for the Canadian tenor.

Based on Virgil's epic poem *The Aeneid*, the opera was said to have preoccupied its French composer, Hector Berlioz, from his childhood. No wonder the behemoth had gained the reputation of being one of opera's most challenging productions to mount. Staging (five hours and numerous sets) and vocally taxing, most notably for the tenor role of Aeneas, *Les Troyens* took its toll.

New York Times music critic Anthony Tommasini explained the vocal technicality for tenors singing the role: "it combines such different styles of singing: heroic passages where Aeneas must slice through Berlioz's orchestra with the power and ping of a Wagnerian tenor, yet also stretches of refined, French-styled lyricism."[103]

Paul had sung the role in 1989 in the Nice, France production and had survived to tell the tale. Nice's opera house, seating around 1,000, had been kind acoustically, and the audience was complimentary. And now he had an opportunity to reprise the role in the cavernous Met—four times the size of Nice, and without amplification. It would be a challenge—one that had been turned down by other less-determined operatic voices. "But I was confident that I was up to it." A number of friends and relatives from Ontario would be in the audience to witness his triumph.

Strong and confident until the first intermission, Paul returned to his dressing room, feeling under the weather. "My throat was feeling tight. Was I coming down with a cold? Or laryngitis? Or was it nerves? Nerves that said that my voice wasn't up to the task?"

As the second act progressed, Paul's confidence was draining away. "At the second intermission, I told the Met's manager: 'I'm not sure I can carry on.'" "We have the understudy here to take over if you can't," the manager answered. More than once in his career being the one who takes over—from an ailing voice, a failing spirit or a diminished confidence—Paul now found himself in the same desperate position. "It had never happened that I was the one to pull out before. I was pretty upset."

Part 13: A Career Disappointment and a Well-Deserved Honor

The tenor left the Metropolitan Opera building dejected and doubt-filled. "I was devastated, and I second-guessed myself for a long time afterwards. Was it nerves that got me down? Or had it been an illness? No matter, this was a wound that never healed." And to add to Paul's feeling of defeat was the long-term result. "The Met never called on me again." He calls it "the biggest disappointment of my career."

58

Before I Get Too Old

As early as 1992, Paul was contemplating the "ever after." The "ever after," after opera, that is. To *Guelph Mercury* columnist Scott Tracey he'd offered: "I do not want to get old in this profession, but I've seen more and more people say that and they can't quit when the time comes . . . I hope I will know when the time comes."[104] But that time hadn't come—yet. Despite some disappointments the preceding year, opera life was still a candy store.

Paul had completed his Bayreuth *Lohengrin* run in 1993, having performed the role over six consecutive summers (*Lohengrin* was not part of the *Festspiele* playbill in 1992). With his last *Lohengrin* in 1997 in Berlin, he had sung the role 250 times.

"I had pretty well sung *Lohengrin* all over the world. So my appeal was lessening and I was receiving fewer offers to sing it." That was quite acceptable. "With *Lohengrin*, I'd achieved everything I wanted to achieve." To compensate, there were new challenges on the horizon. And that some were coming from Canada made the treat sweeter.

Paul's younger brother Ken Frey, a singer in his own right, had approached Kitchener-Waterloo Philharmonic conductor, Howard Dyck, with a musical proposal. Both Ken and Paul had studied with Howard at the WLU Summer Music Workshop in the early 1970's and Howard had gone on to greater achievements: as guest orchestra conductor in Vienna, Salzburg, Prague, and China, among others. He had also been host of CBC Radio's long-running classical music program, *Saturday Afternoon at the Opera*. To his supreme delight, he had also traveled to Bayreuth at the request of the CBC to interview Paul, starring in his first *Lohengrin*.

Part 13: A Career Disappointment and a Well-Deserved Honor

Ken Frey's golden idea was to gather a number of talented musicians and singers from the Kitchener-Waterloo area and produce a CD, the profits from which would be donated to worthy charitable causes. Howard was keen on the idea and over the next period of time looked for commitment to participate. He approached Paul Frey and was thrilled to have his commitment.

And so in 1994, the Consort Caritatis Choir and Orchestra was born.[105] Over the next several years the group toured both in Europe and North America as well as releasing a number of recordings. Paul gladly took his place as lead tenor soloist. Howard recalls Paul's participation in his labor of love.

"Paul was, of course, the biggest star of the group. But you could never have known that. Always humble, cooperative, and congenial, he didn't ever grumble when some of the dressing rooms were below par." Recalling the country boy who struggled to find middle C on a piano and whose sight-reading abilities were virtually non-existent, Howard recalls: "He had no idea how great his voice was, even then. It was an exceptional instrument."[106]

As the new millennium opened, Paul Frey was approaching sixty. And if he continued to sing professionally, he'd need to be satisfied with "character roles." These depended more on acting than on voice. He'd also taken on a modern opera, *Dreyfus*, as a favor to a friend and found that less than satisfying. "You'd take the considerable time and energy to learn the part. And usually modern operas are quite complicated. Then you'd perform it five or six times and it was gone, forgotten. It was never staged again."

An even darker scenario was what some opera stars had opted for as they approached their sixties, when the timbre and strength of the voice had faded. "I'd seen them almost down on their hands and knees begging for a part. They couldn't move on; and it was pathetic to see."

There was no way he was going to follow that path.

And so, Canada beckoned. The Frey family had continued their connection to home—Waterloo Region, and began to make plans to retire there. They'd purchased a condominium in Waterloo in 2001 and Paul used that location as a jumping-off point for the offers that continued—though lessened—to sing. By now he was performing more concerts and oratorios: some in Canada, and a number in one of his favorite venues, Buenos Aires. Europe still called on him too.

But city life, even in bucolic Waterloo, wasn't for the long term. Paul's heart was drawing him back to where his ancestors had settled almost 200 years before. This was "Mennonite country," the St. Clements, Heidelberg, St. Jacobs area north of the urban sprawl. A 160-acre parcel of land he owned was waiting to be lived on and farmed.

Then tragedy struck. Paul's older brother Amsey passed away in 2003 and his home and property, just north of the village of St. Clements, needed a keeper. Amsey's widow did not wish to remain. A decision was made that he and Linda would buy Amsey's home and property. They'd then rent out the parcel of land.

The way to a dignified retirement now seemed clear. Retired opera star Paul Frey would become a gentleman farmer. It was just up to him when this new gig would start.

59

An Honor Bestowed

WHILE PAUL FREY WAS winding down his career in Europe, two old friends from his Waterloo early days were ensuring that he would not slip into retirement obscurely.

Daniel Lichti, who had shared an unrewarding year at the University of Toronto Opera School with Paul in 1975, and was now a successful operatic singer in his own right, as well as a faculty member of the Department of Music at Wilfrid Laurier University, had been working on a tribute to his old friend. With Paul's former voice teacher, Victor Martens, Lichti had put Paul's name forward to receive an honorary doctorate degree from the university. Humbly, Paul accepted the nomination. The degree would be conferred on him at the spring 2002 convocation ceremonies at the university.

In Daniel Lichti's citation to the graduating class, he lauds Paul Frey as: "a man who continues to mirror the humility and strength of the community that he grew up in. A man, who having breathed the rarified air of the operatic world, has returned to his rural Waterloo county roots to indulge in semi-retirement, his love for the farm he never gave up."[107]

And now it was Paul's turn to shine as he rose to give the address to the graduating students. To me, his biographer, he noted his nervousness in giving this address. "I was always uncomfortable when I was out there" (a reference to those with more education than himself). Giving the convocation address to 700 students was surely as "out there" as they come! But as he had before, when called on to step outside his comfort zone, Paul Frey, now Dr. Paul Frey, Doctor of Letters, rose to the challenge.

"To whom much is given, much is expected. All of us here today have been blessed immensely. Even those of you who have student loans to pay back are immensely rich, rich in knowledge, knowledge with which you can make out of life what you desire. This knowledge, whether it be to create wealth, art, science, medicine, or technology, must be passed on, and must be shared."[108]

Paul's last public performance was befittingly a Wagner concert in Barcelona, Spain. A number of friends and family members were present. "And then I just stopped," he states. "No fanfare, no announcement, no farewell tour. I just didn't take any more engagements."

One month later in April 2005, Paul and Linda Frey[109] closed the door of their house in Burg, Switzerland (now sold to another family) and boarded a plane for Toronto, Canada. They were home to stay.

Epilogue

Back Where He Started

(2005–2020)

A LEISURELY DRIVE THROUGH the sleepy villages of St. Clements, Heidelberg, Hawkesville, Wallenstein, and Crosshill, a few kilometers north of the sprawl of a booming Waterloo, Ontario, takes one a step back in time. Driving along Hergott Road, St. Clements's main north-south thoroughfare, you'll pass horse-and-buggy Mennonites, singly or in an orderly convoy heading to Sunday morning service. It's a timeless image. Save for the red caution triangle prominently attached to the rear of the buggy, these Old Order Mennonites and Amish endure more than a century and a half after Paul Frey's ancestors settled here.

A citizen of the world from the late 1970's to early 2000, Paul returned here when it was time to say goodbye to fame.

Spring 2020 will mark fifteen years since Paul and Linda Frey's permanent return to Canada. The transition to country life from the lights and sounds of Bayreuth, the Met, Covent Garden, and La Scala was relatively smooth for this opera star. He'd arranged it that way, in the same meticulous fashion that he'd followed the "five-year plans" during his halcyon days.

"I knew that going from working and traveling pretty well 350 of 365 days a year to nothing could have been awful—very, very difficult. So I did it gradually, taking fewer and fewer jobs between 2000 and 2005." (Paul's list of engagements shows that between 2000 and 2005 he took twenty performances, only one of them an opera, his favorite *Fidelio* given in 2003 in

Buenos Aires.) This contrasts to 1990 when he skipped over time zones, fulfilling twenty-five engagements.

While Paul's "slowing down" transition was wise planning psychologically, it was tough on his voice—even tougher than being overstretched during his glory days. "Keeping your voice strong, flexible, and powerful is difficult, almost impossible when you are not working with it daily. And once you lose the voice," he advises, "it is a challenge to come back."

To stave off stage withdrawal, he made sure to keep busy in retirement. Ironically, that meant a return to farming. "So I partnered with a local farmer and we sharecropped my 160 acres," says Paul. "It was fun and it kept me busy."

His life coming to full circle is not lost on him, now in his late seventies. "At age fourteen, when I left school, I had no desire to work on the farm. All I could think of were trucks, trucks, and more trucks! And here I was, a farmer again."

Opera, so long an integral part of his life, would still remain, but at a distance. The tenor now would be an audience member at operas, not at center stage. He was taken aback, in those early retirement days, with how difficult a transition this would be. "Sitting in the audience and listening to opera was very difficult. It wasn't so much that I wanted to be up there. It was just not at all enjoyable for me." The live music experience has improved for him, and with Toronto only an hour to the east, there is opportunity to indulge.

One half-hour west is the Stratford Festival and the Freys enjoy its wide variety of summertime performances. Especially when son Ben and his wife, Lucy, now living in Morocco, come to visit. "Never long enough for us," he admits.

And when he's at home—his very favorite place to be after years of a jet-setting life—he's tending his immaculate property, just outside the village of St. Clements. "No dandelions allowed," he laughs. Paul's in charge of maintaining the expansive lawns, while Linda tends to the flowerbeds.

As for picking up the thread of old friends after being "in the world" for almost thirty years? No problem here. As early as *Lohengrin* Bayreuth, 1988, Paul was thinking ahead to his "what comes after?" At that time, *Globe and Mail* journalist Robert Everett-Green reported: "he expects ultimately to return to Heidelberg, Ontario, the Mennonite community near Kitchener where he grew up and still owns a farm." Everett-Green quotes

Part 13: A Career Disappointment and a Well-Deserved Honor

Paul as saying: "My best friends and the people that I knew when I was growing up are still there. And I've kept up the contact quite well."[110]

At the time of that interview, less than a dozen years after resettling in Europe, only a thin thread of doubt had peeked out of that self-confidence. "But my occupation and my life here has changed me and sometimes I wonder if it will work out going back—it's such a drastic step."

As 2020 beckons, Paul Frey does keep the friends he'd made when he was only beginning to discover his teenage tenor voice in the St. Jacobs Mennonite church. Twice-weekly golf games in the summer and bowling in the winter keeps him fit and trim, only a few pounds over the weight when he was running up and down the hills of San Francisco and jogging through Central Park in Manhattan. He's made only one concession to age, and a tender knee. "I've started to take a golf cart instead of walking through the course," he admits.

It seems fitting that Paul Frey has returned "home" to retire. He credits his heritage not only with giving him his start musically but with allowing him to survive in the often cutthroat world of entertainment.

"In the long run, I think the way I was brought up helped me as an artist—I always try to sing for the people—to really give them my roles, not just send notes at them. And at home we were taught that it's better to wait until people say good things about you than to do it yourself."

For this writer, it's been so easy to say good things about Paul Frey.

Endnotes

1. Frey and Wideman, *Genealogy of the Frey Family*, 3.
2. Bender and Harder, "Conrad Grebel."
3. Loserth, "Jakob Hutter."
4. Krahn and Dyck, "Menno Simons."
5. Krahn and Dyck, "Menno Simons."
6. Burkholder et al., "Ontario (Canada)."
7. Burkholder, *Brief History of the Mennonites in Ontario*, n.p.
8. Cressman, "Waterloo County (Ontario, Canada)."
9. Eby, *Biographical History of Waterloo Township*.
10. Eby, *Biographical History of Waterloo Township*.
11. "History of Woolwich Township."
12. "History of Woolwich Township."
13. Both Frey sisters would graduate from high school. Lena became a registered nurse and Alice a teacher.
14. At the end of his grade nine year, Ken Frey informed his father that he wished neither to farm nor work in the family trucking business. He wanted to continue on with his education. John Frey was agreeable to this, with Ken's promise to help part-time in both businesses if and when he was needed. John paid for his son's university education till he was twenty-one. Ken went on to achieve his undergraduate and post-graduate EdD degree.
15. Paul's older brother Amsey worked on the family farm under the same terms. He was not paid a salary but his needs and wants were taken care of. And like Paul with the trucking business, Amsey was slated to eventually own the farm business.
16. Guiguet, "Paul Frey Reaches Opera Pinnacle," 17.
17. Over the coming years, there would be other changes in the group. When Winston Martin left the group to attend university in the U.S., Clare Bauman took his place. When Wilf Brubacher left the group, Paul took his place. When Paul left in 1971, Gord Davis replaced him. Marilyn Cook was then added as accompanist.
18. Paul Berg led the Schneider Male Chorus from 1947 to 1975. He was succeeded by Fred Lehman, who remained until 1989. Since 1989, the Schneider Male Chorus has been led by a female conductor: Laurie Rowbotham between 1989 and 2009, and Nancy Kidd from 2009 to present.

Endnotes

19. The 2019–2020 season saw the Schneider Male Chorus celebrating its eighty-second year. Today membership usually ranges between thirty-five and forty men. They continue to perform (primarily locally) between four and eight concerts, raising funds for worthy local charities. The chorus also commits to entertaining at area retirement homes and long-term care facilities.
20. Pratt, "Young St. Jacobs Tenor Festival Star on Wednesday."
21. Pitcher, "Schneider Male Choir Marks Jubilee in 1972."
22. "Waterloo Lutheran University Fonds."
23. Interview with Elizabeth Straus, February 2019.
24. Pitcher, "Characterizations Are Effective."
25. Pitcher, "Trucker Sets Sights on Opera."
26. Interview with Howard Dyck, December 2018.
27. Interview with Raffi Armenian, January 2019.
28. Pitcher, "Choirs Draw Record Crowd to WLU."
29. Pitcher, "Schneider Male Choir Marks Jubilee in 1972."
30. Interview with Raffi Armenian, November 2019.
31. Kraglund, "Forrester Vocally Perfect in Carmen Role."
32. Pitcher, "Frey Development Shown in Conrad Grebel Debut."
33. Pitcher, "Kitchener Tenor Praised by Music Professor," 14.
34. Interview with Daniel Lichti, February 2019.
35. Herb Michaels, "Standing Ovation for Symphony."
36. Kraglund, "Werther's Passion and Beauty Electrify Audience," 17.
37. Kraglund, "Werther's Passion and Beauty Electrify Audience," 17.
38. Kirby, "Tenor Was a Truck Driver Just Like Lanza."
39. Kirby, "Tenor Was a Truck Driver Just Like Lanza."
40. "Mastersinger Paul Frey," *Adrienne Clarkson Presents*, December 1990.
41. Pitcher, "K-W Singers Show Poise in Opera," 14.
42. Kirby, "Tenor Was a Truck Driver Just Like Lanza."
43. It appears that Paul Frey's slight of his alma mater still carries weight. He is not listed in the opera school's list of notable graduates.
44. Interview with Daniel Lichti, January 2019.
45. O'Grady, "La Traviata Gleams in Hands of Canadians."
46. Rudolph, "'Traviata' the Best in 20 Years."
47. Kraglund, "Feeling Rewards in Verdi's Il Corsano."
48. Canada Council for the Arts, https://canadacouncil.ca/.
49. Pitcher, "Tenor Paul Frey Chosen."
50. See: Scott-Stoddard, "Fach System"; "Opera Voices"; DeWood, "Fach System."
51. Kraglund, "La Traviata."
52. Kraglund, "La Traviata."
53. Critics would come to credit Paul Frey's "unaccented" Canadian speech with giving him superior operatic diction and pronunciation.
54. Interview with Rainer Altorfer, February 2019.
55. Interview with Rainer Altorfer, February 2019.
56. Durichen, "Paul Frey: St. Jacob's Businessman."

Endnotes

57. Interview with Patricia Kadvan, December 2018.
58. Interview with Martin Markun, December, 2018.
59. Interview with Martin Markun, December, 2018.
60. Interview with Rainer Altorfer, March 2019.
61. See: "Richard Wagner"; Cooke, "Richard Wagner"; "List of Compositions by Richard Wagner."
62. Interview with Werner Herzog, November 2018.
63. See: Fox, "Peter Hofmann . . . Dies at 66"; Millington, "Peter Hoffman Obituary."
64. Guiguet, "Paul Frey Reaches Opera Pinnacle," 14.
65. Guiguet, "Paul Frey Reaches Opera Pinnacle," 16.
66. Durichen, "Paul Frey: St. Jacobs Businessman," C3.
67. Durichen, "Paul Frey: St. Jacobs Businessman," C3.
68. Durichen, "Paul Frey: St. Jacobs Businessman," C3.
69. Guiguet, "Paul Frey Reaches Opera Pinnacle," 14.
70. Verdino-Süllwold, "We Need a Hero!," 10.
71. Verdino-Süllwold, "We Need a Hero!," 12.
72. Guiguet, "Paul Frey Reaches Opera Pinnacle," 14.
73. Williams, *John Vickers, a Hero's Life*.
74. Citron, "Tenor Traded Hockey for World Stage."
75. Kaptainis, "From a Trucker to a Tenor," D1–D2.
76. Kaptainis, "From a Trucker to a Tenor," D1–D2.
77. Interview with Werner Herzog, February 2019.
78. Everett-Green, "Canadian Tenor Shines," C1.
79. Everett-Green, "Canadian Tenor Shines," C1.
80. Henahan, "Logengrin [*sic*] Staged by Herzog," 11.
81. Everett-Green, "Canadian Tenor Shines," C1.
82. Krawchyk, "World Stage Opens Wide," E3.
83. Krawchyk, "World Stage Opens Wide," E3.
84. Waits for up to five years or more were usual for new Bayreuth ticket purchasers.
85. Krawchyk, "World Stage Opens Wide," E3.
86. Williams, *Jon Vickers, a Hero's Life*, 86.
87. Everett-Green "Finding New Independence," C4.
88. Paul fulfilled this wish by singing Siegmund in *Die Walküre* ten times. He did not sing *Tristan und Isolde* in an opera production.
89. Durichen, "Paul Frey: St. Jacobs Businessman," C3.
90. Kaptainis, "From a Trucker to a Tenor," D1.
91. Kaptainis, "From a Trucker to a Tenor," D1.
92. Kaptainis, "From a Trucker to a Tenor," D1.
93. Everett-Green, "Finding New Independence," C8.
94. "Berlin Wall," https://www.history.com/topics/cold-war/berlin-wall.
95. The Berlin Wall fell shortly after Paul Frey's engagement.
96. Williams, *Jon Vickers, a Hero's Life*, 86.

Endnotes

97. Krawchyk, "Hometown Stage the Most Nerve-Wracking."

98. In 1999, Adrienne Clarkson was named Canada's twenty-sixth governor-general. She held that prestigious post until 2006.

99. Interview with Ben Heppner, May 2019.

100. Tracey, "For Opera Singer Paul Frey," 6B.

101. The oratorio is a large-scale production for orchestra and voice. It usually follows a religious or narrative theme and is enacted without costumes, scenery, or action. Well-known examples are Handel's *Messiah* and Haydn's *Creation*.

102. Littler, "Tenor Wins International Fame."

103. Tommasini, "Les Troyens with Bryan Humel."

104. Tracey, "Audience of Friends Is Tougher!," 6B.

105. Consort Caritatis released six CDs between 1994 and 2003. Their efforts saw them donating $219,000 to Habitat for Humanity and the Mennonite Central Committee.

106. Interview with Howard Dyck, April 2019.

107. Lichti, introduction to Paul Frey honorary doctorate.

108. Frey, convocation address.

109. Ben Frey, age twenty-nine when his parents returned to Canada, graduated from a Swiss university and elected to remain in Europe. He jokes that "my parents left me, rather than the other way around."

110. Everett-Green, "Canadian Tenor Shines in Brilliant Lohengrin."

Bibliography

Personal Interviews

Raffi Armenian, January 2019.
Rainer Altorfer, February 2019.
Howard Dyck, December 2018.
Ben Frey, April 2019.
Ken Frey, March 2019.
Ben Heppner (via email), May 2019.
Werner Herzog, February 2019.
Patricia Kadvan, December 2018.
Daniel Lichti, February 2019.
Martin Markun, February 2019
Elizabeth Straus, April 2019.

Books

Burkholder, L. J. *A Brief History of the Mennonites in Ontario*. Kitchener: Mennonite Conference of Ontario, 1935.
Eby, Ezra E. *A Biographical History of Waterloo Township and Other Townships of the County, Being a History of the Early Settlers and Their Descendants Mostly all of Pennsylvania Dutch Origin, and Also Other Unpublished Historical Information Chiefly of a Local Character*. 2 vols. Berlin, ON, 1895, 1896.
English, John, and Kenneth McLaughlin. *Kitchener: An Illustrated History*. Waterloo, ON: Wilfrid Laurier, 1983.
Frey, Levi, and Elizabeth Wideman. *Genealogy of the Frey Family, 1772 to 1965*.
Tiessen, Hildegard Froese, and Paul Gerard Tiessen. *Waterloo County Landscapes, 1930-966*. St. Jacobs, ON: Sand Hills, 1986.
Williams, Jeannie. *Jon Vickers: A Hero's Life*, Boston: Northern University Press, 1999.

Bibliography

Periodicals

Citron, Paula. "Tenor Traded Hockey for World Stage." *Montreal Star*, n.d.
Durichen, Pauline. "Paul Frey: St. Jacobs Businessman Moves to the Top of the Opera World." *Kitchener-Waterloo Record*, September 24, 1987.
Everett-Green, Robert. "Finding New Independence on the Road to Success." *Globe and Mail*, August 24, 1988, C4.
———. "Canadian Tenor Shines in Brilliant Lohengrin." *Globe and Mail*, August 25, 1988.
Guiget, Kristin Marie. "Paul Frey Reaches Opera Pinnacle." *Music Magazine*, September/October 1986.
Henahan, Donal. "Logengrin [sic] Staged by Herzog." *New York Times*, August 3 1987.
Kaptainis Arthur. "From a Trucker to a Tenor." *Montreal Gazette*, October 10, 1987.
Kirby, Blake. "The Tenor Was a Truck Driver Just Like Lanza." *Globe and Mail*, January 12, 1976.
Kraglund, John. "Forrester Vocally Perfect in Carmen Role." *Globe and Mail*, February 5, 1973.
———. "Feeling Rewards in Verdi's Il Corsano." *Globe & Mail*, February 1977.
———. "La Traviata." *Globe and Mail*, April 13, 1978.
———. "Werther's Passion and Beauty Electrify Audience." *Globe and Mail*, October 12, 1975.
Krawchyk, Ed. "World Stage Opens Wide to Canadian Singer." *London Free Press*, August 22, 1987.
———. "Hometown Stage the Most Nerve-Wracking." *London Free Press*, May 23, 1989.
Littler, William. "Tenor Wins International Fame for Canada." *Toronto Star*, September 1987.
Michaels, Herb. "Standing Ovation for Symphony." *Mississauga News*, March 3, 1975.
O'Grady, Terence. "La Traviata Gleams in Hands of Canadians." From PF clipping collection, n.d.
Pitcher, W. J. "Characterizations Are Effective in WLU's Scenes from Opera." *Kitchener-Waterloo Record*, August 13, 1971.
———. "Choirs Draw Record Crowd to WLU." *Kitchener-Waterloo Record*, n.d.
———. "Frey Development Shown in Conrad Grebel Debut." *Kitchener-Waterloo Record*, March 13, 1973.
———. "Kitchener Tenor Praised by Music Professor. *Kitchener-Waterloo Record*, May 24, 1973.
———. "K-W Singers Show Poise in Opera/" *Kitchener-Waterloo Record*, April 4, 1974.
———. "Schneider Male Choir Marks Jubilee in 1972." *Kitchener-Waterloo Record*, December 24, 1971.
———. "Tenor Paul Frey Chosen: 5 Canadians win Auditions in Europe." *Kitchener-Waterloo Record*, n.d.
———. "Trucker Sets Sights on Opera." *Kitchener-Waterloo Record*, n.d.
Pratt, Michael T. "Young St. Jacobs Tenor Festival Star on Wednesday." *Kitchener-Waterloo Record*, 1966.
Rudolph, Jack. "'Traviata' the Best in 20 Years." *Green Bay News Chronicle*, January 18, 1977.
Tommasini, Anthony. "Les Troyens with Bryan Humel at the Metropolitan Opera." *New York Times*, December 27, 2012.

Bibliography

Tracey, Scott. "For Opera Singer Paul Frey... an Audience of Friends Is Tougher!" *Guelph Daily Mercury*, April 30, 1992.

Verdino-Sullwold, Carla Maria. "We Need a Hero! The Evolution of the Heldentenor." *Music Magazine*, November/December 1988.

Internet Sources

Bender, Harold S., and Leland D. Harder. "Conrad Grebel, (ca. 1498–1526)." *Global Anabaptist Mennonite Encyclopedia Online*. 1989. https://gameo.org/index.php?title=Grebel,_Conrad_(ca._1498-1526).

"Berlin Wall." History.com. November 9, 2019. https://www.history.com/topics/cold-war/berlin-wall.

"The Bayreuth Festival—Bayreuther Festspiele." http://www.wagneropera.net/bayreuth/index.htm.

Burkholder, Paul H., John M. Bender, and Sam Steiner. "Ontario (Canada)." *Global Anabaptist Mennonite Encyclopedia Online*. 1990. https://gameo.org/index.php?title=Ontario_(Canada).

"Canada Council for the Arts: Bringing the Arts to Life." https://canadacouncil.ca/.

Canadian Opera Company. http://www.coc.ca.

Cooke, Deryck V. "Richard Wagner." *Encyclopædia Britannica*. February 9, 2020. https://www.britannica.com/biography/Richard-Wagner-German-composer.

Cressman, Boyd J. "Waterloo County (Ontario, Canada)." *Global Anabaptist Mennonite Encyclopedia Online*. 1959. http://gameo.org/index.php?title=Waterloo_County_(Ontario,_Canada).

DeWood, Dale. "The Fach System: Origin, Function, and the Dangers of Perception." https://www.academia.edu/32108110/The_Fach_System_origin_function_and_the_dangers_of_perception.

Fox, Margalit. "Peter Hofmann, Singer of Rock, Opera and Musicals, Dies at 66." December 1, 2010. https://www.nytimes.com/2010/12/01/arts/music/01hofmann.html.

Harvey, Jocelyn. "Canada Council for the Arts." *Canadian Encyclopedia*, March 4, 2015. https://www.thecanadianencyclopedia.ca/en/article/canada-council-for-the-arts.

"History of Woolwich Township." https://www.woolwich.ca/en/doing-business/HIstory.aspx.

Krahn, Cornelius, and Cornelius J. Dyck. "Menno Simons (1496–1561)." *Global Anabaptist Mennonite Encyclopedia Online*. 1990. http://gameo.org/index.php?title=Menno_Simons_(1496-1561).

"List of Compositions by Richard Wagner." https://www.revolvy.com/page/List-of-compositions-by-Richard-Wagner.

Loserth, Johann. "Jakob Hutter, (d. 1536)." *Global Anabaptist Mennonite Encyclopedia Online*. 1959. http://gameo.org/index.php?title=Hutter,_Jakob_(d._1536).

Millington, Barry. "Peter Hoffman Obituary." *The Guardian*, December 2, 2010. https://www.theguardian.com/music/2010/dec/02/peter-hofmann-obituary.

Morris, Christopher, and Carl Morey. Canadian Opera Company. *Canadian Encyclopedia*, March 4, 2015. https://www.thecanadianencyclopedia.ca/en/article/canadian-opera-company-emc.

"Opera Voices: The Basic Fachs." The Opera 101. https://www.theopera101.com/operaabc/voices.

Bibliography

"Richard Wagner." ArkivMusic, 2018. http://www.arkivmusic.com/classical/Name/Richard-Wagner/Composer/12732-31.

Schneider Male Chorus. http:www.schneidermalechorus.ca.

Scott-Stoddart. Nina. "The Fach System of Vocal Classification." http://halifaxsummeroperafestival.com/?page_id=3270.

"60 Years with the Canadian Opera Company." CBC Digital Archives. https://www.cbc.ca/archives/topic/60-years-with-the-canadian-opera-company.

Other

Frey, Paul. Convocation address. Wilfrid Laurier University, spring convocation, 2002.

Lichti, Daniel. Introduction to Paul Frey honorary doctorate. Wilfrid Laurier University, spring convocation, 2002.

"Mastersinger Paul Frey." *Adrienne Clarkson Presents*, December, 1990.

"Waterloo Lutheran University Fonds." Press release, May 31, 1971.

CPSIA information can be obtained
at www.ICGtesting.com
Printed in the USA
BVHW040255041120
592458BV00006B/74